THE EAT-A-BUG COOKBOOK

THE EAT-A-BUG COOKBOOK

REVISED

40 ways to cook crickets, grasshoppers, ants,
water bugs, spiders, centipedes, and their kin

DAVID GEORGE GORDON

Photographs by Chugrad McAndrews
Illustrations by Karen Luke Fildes

TEN SPEED PRESS
Berkeley

DEDICATION

**To my brother, Stuart, who first showed me
that gross can be good, and to Drew and Joe,
for showing me just how good it could be**

A previous edition was published in the United States by Ten Speed Press,
Berkeley, in 1998.

Library of Congress Cataloging-in-Publication Data is on file with the publisher.

Trade Paperback ISBN: 978-1-60774-436-8
eBook ISBN: 978-1-60774-437-5

Printed in China

Design by Colleen Cain
Food and prop styling by Anne Treanor Miska

10 9 8 7 6 5 4 3 2 1

Second Edition

CONTENTS

Acknowledgments • ix

Introduction: Embracing Entomophagy • **1**

PART ONE

Don't Worry, Be Hoppy: Nine Culinary Leaps of Faith, Using Crickets, Grasshoppers, and Their Kin

Chapter 1: Cooking with Crickets • **23**

Niblets and Cricklets • 25

Orthopteran Orzo • 27

Chirpy Chex Party Mix • 28

Crispy Crickets • 29

Cricket Seasoning à la Vij's • 30

Bugs in a Rug • 31

Chocolate Cricket Torte • 32

Chapter 2: Grilled Grasshoppers, Creamed Katydids, and Locusts Lovingly Prepared • 33

    Cream of Katydid Soup • 35

    Oaxacan Whoppers • 36

    St. John's Bread • 38

    Sheesh! Kabobs • 41

    Really Hoppin' John • 43

    Chapulines con Chocolate Fondue • 45

PART TWO
Togetherness: A Selection of Social Insects for Special Occasions

Chapter 3: Tantalizing Termites (The Other White Meat) • 49

    Curried Termite Stew • 52

    Termite Treats • 53

Chapter 4: Beginning with Bees • 54

    Glory Bee • 57

    Three Bee Salad • 59

    Bee's Knees • 60

Chapter 5: Ants On (and In) the House • 61

    Ant Jemima's Buckwheat-Bug Griddlecakes • 63

    Amaretto Honeypots • 65

    Ants in Pants • 67

    Pear Salad with Chiangbai Ants • 69

PART THREE

Who's Buggin' Whom? Nine Ways to Turn the Tables on Household and Garden Pests

Chapter 6: Preparing Pantry Pests • 75

Cockroach à la King • 78

Larval Latkes (a.k.a. Grubsteaks) • 80

Chapter 7: Garden Grazers Alfresco • 81

Wasabi Wax Worms • 83

Superworm Tempura with Plum Dipping Sauce • 84

Fried Green Tomato Hornworms • 87

Piz-zz-zz-za • 88

Pest-o • 90

Alpha-Bait Soup • 91

White Chocolate and Wax Worm Cookies • 93

PART FOUR

Side Orders: A Smorgasbord of Treats from Assorted Arthropod Taxa

Chapter 8: Spineless Delights • 97

Giant Water Bug on Watercress • 100

Watermelon and Water Bug Surprise • 103

Sweet and Sour Silkworm • 105

Ample Drumsticks • 106

Spin-akopita • 108

Sky Prawn • 110

Odonate Hors d'Oeuvres • 112

Scorpion Scaloppine • 113

Party Pupae • 116

Deep-Fried Tarantula Spider • 119

Resources • 120

Index • 124

THE BUTTERFLY'S BALL AND THE GRASSHOPPER'S FEAST

Come, take up your hats, and away let us haste
To the Butterfly's ball and the Grasshopper's feast;
The trumpeter Gad-fly has summon'd the crew,
And the revels are now only waiting for you.
On the smooth-shaved grass by the side of the wood,
Beneath a broad oak that for ages has stood,
See the children of the earth, and tenants of air,
For an evening's amusement together repair.
And there came the Beetle, so blind and so black,
Who carried the Emmet, his friend, on his back;
And there came the Gnat, and the Dragon-fly too,
And all their relations, green, orange, and blue.
And there came the Moth with her plumage of down,
And the Hornet with jacket of yellow and brown,
Who with him the Wasp, his companion, did bring;
They promised that evening to lay by their sting.
Then the sly little Dormouse peep'd out of his hole,
And led to the feast his blind cousin the Mole;
And the Snail, with his horns peeping out of his shell,
Came fatigued with the distance, the length of an ell.
A mushroom the table, and on it were spread
A Water-dock-leaf, which their table-cloth made;
The viands were various, to each of their taste,
And the Bee brought the honey to sweeten the feast.
With steps more majestic the Snail did advance,
And he promised the gazers a minuet dance;
But they all laughed so loudly he pulled in his head,
And went in his own little chamber to bed.
Then, as the evening gave way to the shadows of night,
Their watchman, the Glow-worm, came out with his light:
So home let us hasten, while yet we can see,
For no watchman is waiting for you or for me.

—William Roscoe (1753–1831)

ACKNOWLEDGMENTS

In the original *Eat-a-Bug Cookbook*, I thanked the many people who helped me, directly or indirectly, in shaping the thirty-three recipes in that book. And here I am again, fifteen years later, thanking my previous team of able bug suppliers, accomplished chefs, adventurous taste testers, assiduous editors and publishers, and authoritative arthropod lovers for their assistance. They are Mariah Bear, Paul Boyer, Sharon Collman, Lisa Darmo, Florence Dunkel, Don Ehlen, Joe Euro, T-Joe Frank, John Gautreaux, Zack Lemman, David Maxfield, Larry Peterman, Jane Peterson, Braiden Rex-Johnson, Robin Roche, Kristin, Otto, Anna, and John Smith, Louis Sorkin, Sally Sprenger, Scott Stenjem, Barney Tomberlin, and Phil Wood.

Help with this revised and updated edition came from another batch of close friends and associates, freethinkers who share my belief that insects are the food of the future, good for the environment and good for us all. This second group includes Mark Berman, Rena Chen, Mark Dennis, Meeru Dhalwala, Aaron Dossey, Art Evans, Dave Gracer, Dianne Guilfoyle, Harman Johar, Brent Karner, Steve Kutcher, Paul Landkamer, Daniella Martin, Monica Martinez, Leonard Meuse, Julieta Ramos-Elorduy, Marianne Shockley, Renzo Tomlinson, Ger van der Wal, and Rosanna Yau. I thank them for their helpful advice and heartfelt encouragement.

A final outpouring of gratitude goes to those who helped shape the work you now hold in your hands. They include Colleen Cain (book designer), Elizabeth Stromberg (art director), Emily Timberlake (editor), and Aaron Wehner (publisher), and I am indebted to them all. I'm also grateful to photographer Chugrad McAndrews, food stylist Anne Treanor Miska, and my literary agent and longtime friend, Anne Depue.

I am forever appreciative of my beloved bride, Karen Luke Fildes, who contributed the illustrations in this edition and has been extremely supportive of my trip in so many ways. And I applaud my chidren for putting up with me.

Bug appétit!

INTRODUCTION
EMBRACING ENTOMOPHAGY

A Meal Moth in Every Pantry, a Chinch Bug in Every Pot

What's this book about? Eating bugs, of course. Within these pages is everything you'll need to know about bug-based cuisine, plus an assortment of tantalizing bug dishes to tempt—and, at times, intimidate—your family and friends.

By "bugs" I mean all land-dwelling arthropods—insects, spiders, centipedes, millipedes, scorpions, and their kin—that can be caught (or otherwise acquired), cooked, and eaten. This definition may annoy some scientists who believe the word "bug" should be applied only to members of the insect order Hemiptera, the so-called "true bugs," such as aphids or stink bugs, with mouthparts designed for sucking. Entomologically speaking, they may be right; etymologically, however, they are probably missing the point.

Four hundred years ago, when people used the word "bug" they meant a ghost or hobgoblin—a bugaboo. They used the same word to describe the bedbug, another near-invisible spirit in the dark that, incidentally, happens to be a member of the order Hemiptera. Over time, the meaning of the word expanded. Eventually "bug" was applied to all manner of small cold-blooded critters—even flu germs and German-made automobiles.

"Bug" doesn't always have a negative connotation nowadays. I've heard diners in New Orleans call an order of boiled crayfish a plateful of bugs. My friends who are scuba divers also use this term to describe the spiny lobster, a succulent second cousin to both the crayfish and the tiger prawn.

So, why not use the word "bug" to identify the lobster's edible relatives on land? With the sole exception of the water bugs *Lethocerus indicus* and *americanus*, freshwater inhabitants of

North America and Southeast Asia, the bugs described in this book are all terrestrial. Bugs were here many millions of years before us, and, some (including Archie the Cockroach) will inherit the earth long after we're gone. In other words, look elsewhere if you're seeking recipes for shrimp creole, crab Louie, or lobster Thermidor. But read on if you'd like to learn how to make Crispy Crickets, Scorpion Scaloppine, and other surprisingly satisfying fare.

Who Eats Bugs?

Entomophagy (pronounced en-tuh-MOFF-a-gee)—that's bug eating to you—has been practiced for many centuries throughout Africa, Asia, Australia, the Middle East, and North, South, and Central America. And the feasting continues according to Marcel Dicke, professor of entomology at Wageningen University and winner of the Dutch version of the Nobel Prize, with an estimated 80 percent of the world's population eating bugs. Insects and their kin are enjoyed nearly everywhere except for Europe and the United States and Canada. That's right: we're the weirdos for *not* eating bugs.

It's hard to say what motivated some of our forefathers to refrain from this widespread, nutritionally beneficial, and unquestionably wholesome practice. Quite possibly, our current disdain for bug cuisine was shared by the first farmers of northern Europe and, by extension, European colonists in the New World. They regarded most land arthropods, and insects in particular, as crop- and livestock-robbing pests. To these early agronomists, eating bugs was probably akin to sleeping with the enemy. To discourage anyone from going over to the "other side," they manufactured all manner of bad press for bugs. Hundreds of years later, fear-mongering pest control companies took the insect hate ball and ran with it. In their eyes, the only good bug was a dead one. Nowadays, most people in Europe and North America regard insects and other land arthropods as unclean, germ-laden, and foul tasting—three views that have little, if any, basis in fact.

Many of the world's indigenous people still harvest and eat bugs, just as we do artichokes, oysters, and many of the myriad gifts from the land and sea. Did you know, for instance, that when faced with a cloud of locusts, native Algerians will break out the brooms and start

FOOD FOR THOUGHT

Be the life of your next Eat-a-Bug banquet with these astounding facts about terrestrial arthropods:

- Two-thirds of all living animal species are insects.
- A queen termite can live for fifty years. In her prime she can lay two thousand eggs per day.
- Most spiders have eight eyes.
- Scorpions have been around for at least 440 million years.
- If cockroaches were as big as automobiles, they would be able to sprint at speeds in excess of 150 miles per hour.
- There are more kinds of insects in one tropical rainforest tree than in the entire state of Vermont.

sweeping their sudden bounty of insects into baskets and bags? Or that honey gatherers in Malaysia will sell the liquid bounty from a wild hive, but they'll save any larval bees still in the honeycomb for themselves? How many of you have heard about the mopane worm business in rural South Africa? The fat, juicy caterpillars of the emperor moth are plucked from the mopane trees at Christmastime, after which they are gutted, dried, and sold at markets.

The first people of North America were avid bug eaters. I've read that members of the Klamath tribe of southeastern Oregon lit fires beneath trees to smoke out the caterpillars of the pandora moth, which would then fall to the forest floor, where the Klamath harvested them for later consumption. One chief is said to have amassed a ton and a half of smoked and dried pandora caterpillars during the summer of 1920.

"I have seen the Cheyennes, Snakes, Utes, etc., eat vermin off each other by the fistful," wrote the nineteenth-century chronicler Father Pierre-Jean De Smet. "Often great chiefs would pull off their shirts in my presence without ceremony, and while they chatted, would amuse themselves with carrying on this branch of the chase in the seams. As fast as they dislodged the game, they crunched it with as much relish as more civilized mouths crack almonds and hazel-nuts or the claws of crabs and crayfishes."

Although entomophagy may have fallen from favor among most of the members of North America's founding tribes, it still thrives in the village markets of Oaxaca and a few other Mexican states. A favorite snack in these locations is *chapulines*, sun-dried grasshopper nymphs sprinkled with salt and seasoned with chile and lime. This delicacy, which originated with the native tribes of southwest Mexico, has been handed down from one generation to the next. The legacy of bug eating is also alive in the heart of Mexico City, where gourmet restaurants specializing in pre-Hispanic cuisine still offer *cazuela de escamoles a la bilbaina*—larval red ants, fried in olive oil and lightly dusted with dry red chile—to their discerning clientele.

> **“** They had another Dish made of a sort of Locusts, whose Bodies were about an Inch and a half long, and as thick as the top of one's little Finger; with large thin Wings, and long and small Legs. At this time of the Year, these Creatures came in great swarms to devour their potato-leaves, and other herbs; and the Natives would go out with small Nets, and take a Quart at one sweep. When they had enough, they would carry them home, and parch them over the Fire in an earthen Pan; and then their Wings and Legs would fall off, and their Heads and Backs would turn red like boil'd Shrimps, before being brownish. Their Bodies being full, would eat very moist, their Heads would crackle in one's Teeth. I did eat once of this Dish, and liked it well enough but their other Dish my Stomach would not take. **”**
> —William Dampier on bug eating in the Bashee Islands, *A New Voyage Round the World* (1687)

The Benefits of Bug Eating

What's to be gained from a diet of bugs? I'm glad you asked, since I've been collecting data on this topic for fifteen years. A grasshopper's body is more than 20 percent protein. Compare this with the protein in lean ground beef (about 27 percent) and you'll see why even professional athletes could sustain themselves on a diet of arthropods. Since grasshoppers and their relatives contain large quantities of water, their protein content jumps to around 60 percent after these animals are dried.

Many protein-rich bugs are also good sources of vitamins, minerals, and fats. Are you worried about warding off osteoporosis? Then eat crickets, which are loaded with calcium. Want to avoid anemia? Try termites; they're rich in iron. One hundred grams of giant silkworm moth larvae provide 100 percent of the daily requirements for copper, zinc, iron, thiamin, and riboflavin. It turns out that animals that eat greens have higher levels of omega-3 fatty acids, the "good" fats with antioxidant powers that can help thwart certain forms of cancer and disease. Many insects contain abundant stores of lysine, an amino acid deficient in the diets of many rural Latin Americans, who rely heavily on corn. Could the ancient Aztecs have known this? They sold corn infested with corn earworm—a small green- and black-striped caterpillar that most modern farmers consider a pest—for more money than corn without the nutritionally supportive bug.

Bug eating is good for the planet, too. Raising cows, pigs, and sheep is a tremendous waste of the planet's resources, but bug

Nutritional Value of Various Insects (per 100 grams)

	Protein (g)	Fat (g)	Carbohydrate (mg)	Calcium (mg)	Iron (mg)
Crickets	12.9	5.5	5.1	75.8	9.5
Grasshoppers (small)	20.6	6.1	3.9	35.2	5.0
Grasshoppers (large)	14.3	3.3	2.2	27.5	3.0
Giant water beetles	19.8	8.3	2.1	43.5	13.6
Red ants	13.9	3.5	2.9	47.8	5.7
Silk worm pupae	9.6	5.6	2.3	41.7	1.8
Termites	14.2	n/a	n/a	0.050	35.5
Weevils	6.7	n/a	n/a	0.186	13.1
For comparison:					
Beef (Lean Ground)	27.4	5.0	n/a	0.012	3.5
Fish (Broiled Cod)	28.5	1.0	n/a	0.031	1.0

Source: Data collected by Jared Ostrem and John VanDyk for the Entomology Department of Iowa State University.

ranching is pretty benign. It all comes down to what food scientists call the efficiency of conversion (ECI) of ingested food, a way of rating how metabolically thrifty different kinds of animals are. ECI ratings are derived by measuring the weight that an animal gains from eating an established weight of food. Chickens, which produce thirty-eight to forty pounds of meat from one hundred pounds of feed, get a fairly high ECI rating—around 38 or 40. By comparison, beef cattle and sheep are real losers, producing ECI values of 10 and 5.3, respectively. Another way of looking at this: 90 percent of a steer's diet and 95 percent of a sheep's are wasted, at least from the meat consumer's perspective.

Accurate ECI values for insects are difficult to obtain. However, the ratings that are available are certainly respectable: 19 to 31 for silkworm caterpillars, 16 to 37 for the pale western cutworm, and up to 44 for German cockroaches. In addition, few if any harmful effects are associated with the commercial cultivation of these arthropods for food.

Comparatively food- and water-efficient livestock such as chickens and hogs (with ECI values of 17 to 20, respectively) also have drawbacks. Operations to raise both animals have the potential to generate large quantities of waste, which, if managed improperly, can pollute rivers and lakes, degrading our water supplies. Furthermore, the reserves of fresh water needed for rearing livestock are limited. It takes about 2,600 gallons of water over the course of the animal's lifetime to produce 1 pound of beef. Alternatively, some insects such as the

mealworm, which are commonly sold as live food for pets, can grow to maturity without a single sip of water. These metabolically thrifty organisms get all the moisture they need from the few molecules of water in their otherwise bone-dry food.

In 2010 Arnold van Huis, Marcel Dicke, and several other Dutch scientists looked at the volume of methane and nitrous oxide linked to manure and flatulence from farm-raised cows and pigs. They compared this amount with the volume of gases produced by lab-reared mealworms, crickets, locusts, sun beetles, and cockroaches. Results from the Dutch study revealed that insects grew more rapidly and gave off less stinky gas than their mammalian counterparts.

Curbing emissions of methane and nitrous oxide—two of the more common greenhouse gases—is of vital importance to our planet's well-being. Eighteen percent of greenhouse gas emissions can be traced to cow farts and pig poop. Just think about it: that's a bigger share than produced by all the world's cars, trucks, and motorcycles combined. The large but lightweight molecules of methane and nitrous oxide drift skyward and eventually enter the earth's upper atmosphere. Here they form a dense layer that, much like the glass panes in an old-fashioned greenhouse, allow sunlight to penetrate but will not let go of any residual heat.

This greenhouse effect is causing the earth to gradually warm, which is wreaking havoc on weather patterns, causing glaciers to melt, and creating drought conditions that could lead to food shortages in many parts of the

ENTO-EPHEMERA

Chitin (pronounced KYE-tin) covers every bit of a land arthropod's body, even the eyes. It's nearly as tough as horn and about as flexible as our fingernails. When a growing insect, centipede, or spider needs more room, it must split a seam and step outside this tight-fitting suit.

Temporarily freed from the constraints of the chitin, the young invertebrate will gulp air or take other measures to pump itself up, in some instances, nearly doubling its overall volume. After a while, the chitinous outer wrapper of this newly enlarged arthropod starts to harden. Eventually—perhaps after several hours—the exoskeleton becomes as tough and unyielding as the old armored suit.

world. The Dutch scientists believe that we could someday curb greenhouse gas emissions by as much as 60 percent if we were to tend herds of, say, grasshoppers instead of cattle.

"It's pretty obvious," says Dave Gracer, founder of SmallStock Food Strategies, a purveyor of edible insects based in Providence, Rhode Island. "In terms of the environment, eating insects is like riding a bicycle. Eating a steak is like driving a big gas-guzzling SUV."

Need more reasons to order a bug burger instead of a Big Mac? Then let me point out that many of our common garden pests are edible. If everyone served rapacious critters such as weevils (page 90) and tomato hornworms (page 87) for lunch or dinner, we'd have little need for most over-the-counter pesticide powders and sprays. On a global scale, this could make an incredible difference to the health of the environment and to humankind.

And let's not overlook the good we could do by lessening our reliance on conventional sources of protein—chicken, beef, pork, and fish—and ramping up our consumption of insects, spiders, and other mini-livestock. In doing so, we could greatly reduce the damage being done from persistently overharvesting our oceans and depleting its resources. At the same time, we'd be protecting the few remaining tracts of wilderness that have yet to be cleared to create pastures for beef cows. Global consumption of meat has increased almost threefold since 1970, and that figure is expected to double again by 2050, yet worldwide, 70 percent of all agricultural land is already being used for livestock production. Clearly there isn't enough room on our planet to satisfy the collective demand for beef and similar sources of protein.

That's why in 2008 the Food and Agriculture Organization (FAO) of the United Nations hosted a conference to explore ways of combating world hunger with reliable supplies of farm-reared forest insects. The site of the conference, Chiang Mai, Thailand, is a time-honored locale for the wild harvest of edible insects. "As researchers in northeastern Thailand have discovered, local people consume edible forest insects not because they are environmentally friendly or nutritious—or because they are cheap compared to meat or poultry," wrote the conference's organizers, Patrick Durst and Kenichi Shono. "Rather, they choose to eat insects simply because they taste good!"

Four years later, a follow-up conference on this topic was held at FAO headquarters in Rome. In a related measure, the European Union announced in 2012 that it was making available three million euros (about four million U.S. dollars) for a research project to exploit the potential of insects as alternative sources of protein, in keeping with its Millennium Development Goals.

So you see? I'm in good company by promoting the worldwide consumption of bugs.

Shouldn't Everyone Eat Bugs?

In his persuasively written *Why Not Eat Insects?*, published in 1885, Vincent M. Holt argued that England's starving peasantry would be better fed if they rejected cattle, pigs, and the rest of barnyard life and embraced caterpillars, beetles, and other cold-blooded creatures of forest and field. "People," he wrote, "will enjoy oysters and cockles, while they abominate snails; they will make themselves ill with indigestible and foul-feeding lobsters while they look with horror upon pretty, clean-feeding caterpillars."

The rich could afford to be dainty, observed Holt. But it was everyone's moral obligation to end the suffering of starving laborers by encouraging them to partake of an overlooked and abundant food supply—the bugs of the British Isles.

Holt focused his attention on an assortment of arthropods, all of which were "vegetable feeders, clean, palatable, wholesome,

and decidedly more particular in their feeding than ourselves." He presented two sample menus, each for an eight-course dinner almost entirely derived from locally collected invertebrate fauna.

Far from suggesting simple working-class fare, Holt described Larves de Hanneton Grillées (Deviled Cockchafer Grubs) and Fricassée de Poulets aux Chrysalides (Boiled Neck of Mutton with Wireworm Sauce) as suitable entrées. Alas, no recipes for these delicacies were included in his book. However, he provided his fortunate readers with detailed instructions for preparing at least one item, a sort of wood louse white sauce:

> Collect a quantity of the finest wood-lice to be found (no difficult task, as they swarm under the bark of every rotten tree), and drop them into boiling water, which will kill them instantly, but not turn them red, as might be expected. At the same time put into a saucepan a quarter pound of fresh butter, a teaspoonful of flour, a small glass of water, a little milk, some pepper and salt, and place it on the stove. As soon as the sauce is thick, take it off and put in the wood-lice. This is an excellent sauce for fish. Try it.

The English edible bug enthusiast did everything in his power to convince people that edible insects were where it's at. More than a hundred years after its publication, Holt's book is considered an underground classic. Nonetheless, it has failed to change the rather stolid eating habits of the Brits.

More recently, Holt's cause has gained momentum on the other side of the Atlantic Ocean, thanks in large part to Ronald L. Taylor, the author of what can best be described as the bug-eater's bible, a scholarly 224-page book with a truly inspired title: *Butterflies in My Stomach*. For at least a decade after its release in the 1970s, this book (and its slim companion volume, *Entertaining with Insects*, cowritten by Taylor and one of his students, Barbara Carter) was the only readily available source of information on bug eating for like-minded epicures. Almost forty years after it was first published, you'll still find many references to these books in magazines, academic texts, and food blogs.

It wasn't until 1988, when the *Food Insects Newsletter* arrived on the scene, that the cause of entomophagy moved forward once more. Created by University of Wisconsin entomology professor Gene DeFoliart and edited by Florence Dunkel, a professor of entomology at Montana State University, this quarterly journal provided a lively forum for bug eaters. The journal no longer has a print edition; however, its editors continue to spread the word via their website.

Travels with My Ant: Meet Doris and Wes

With a nappy covering of reddish-brown bristles and a legspan of about eight inches, my pet Chilean rose tarantula, Doris, was my unofficial taste tester for nearly a decade. She would gobble crickets, mealworms, and any other live leftovers from my bug-cooking experiments with zeal. But when she passed away in 2005, I began looking for her replacement.

Doris proved a hard act to follow. I first tried a baby goliath bird-eating spider, the juvenile form of the largest spider species on earth. But I learned only after the might-be-giant arachnid died in an unsuccessful attempt to molt that individuals of this species require more care, including carefully controlled humidity and heat, in order to thrive.

Next I acquired a Texas brown tarantula, captured in, of all places, Roswell, New Mexico, near the alleged site of a 1947 UFO crash. That specimen, named Ernest, proved too feisty, biting whenever he was handled, so I wound up giving him to a couple of dear friends who were okay with this.

In 2012, I purchased Wes, a Mexican rose-gray tarantula spiderling about the size of a Cheerio. Raised on a protein-rich diet of farm-reared crickets and wild-caught pill bugs, Wes has grown rapidly. He has molted six times as of this writing, each time emerging from his cast-off body armor as a bigger, more robust beastie.

Currently, the size of a silver dollar, and likely to exceed Doris in heft someday, the junior mascot of *The Eat-a-Bug Cookbook* is living proof that a diet of bugs has its benefits.

In the past few years some valuable websites and Facebook pages devoted to entomophagy and the rearing of food insects have also popped up. Information on these sites, the newsletter, Taylor's two books, and a few other sources worth perusing is contained in the resources section at the end of this book.

Since the 1990s, people's attitudes about bugs have been changing. On the whole, we've become more appreciative of the entire animal kingdom, not just what we biologists call "charismatic megafauna"—crowd-pleasing animals like lions, tigers, eagles, penguins, dolphins, and whales. This new interest in small wonders has inspired many zoos and museums to add insect festivals and bug fairs to their yearly calendars. Highlights of these well-attended public programs often include displays of edible insects, usually with opportunities for fair-goers to sample dishes made from bugs (a list of such events is contained at the end of the book). As a result, more people each year are indulging in entomophagy, whether at school assemblies, museum-sponsored insect fairs, or elegant five-course dinners. "There's hardly an entomology student alive today who hasn't sampled some sort of insect-based cuisine," claims Florence Dunkel. "And even before college, more and more young people are trying insects in high school or at gatherings of their local 4-H clubs." Entomophagy seems even more relevant now, especially among young adults, than it did when the original *Eat-a-Bug Cookbook* was published in 1998.

So whether you're a youngster or an old-timer like me, seize the moment to expand your diet and exercise your taste buds today. There's a wealth of bugs—about two hundred million for every person alive today—and no shortage of ways to prepare them, as this book demonstrates.

Government-Approved Entomophagy

Few Americans realize that they eat bugs as part of their daily routine. And they're unaware that entomophagy is officially sanctioned by the U.S. Food and Drug Administration, which has established the permissible degrees of insect damage and infestation (that's right, the allowable number of eggs, immature and adult insects, or their parts) for various foods.

The FDA recognizes that it's nearly impossible to keep tiny insects out of items such as spinach, cornmeal, and dried beans, so they've established standards, more for aesthetic reasons than because they're necessary to maintain public health. And they've hired inspectors, arming them with ultra-high-powered microscopes with which to search for the minute signs of tampering by the six-legged set.

From the government's perspective it's okay if there are up to 60 aphids in $3^{1}/_{2}$ ounces of frozen broccoli, perfectly fine if there are 2 or 3 fruit fly maggots in 200 grams of tomato juice. As many as 99 insect fragments are allowed in 25 grams of curry powder, 74 mites in 100 grams of canned mushrooms, 12 or more insect heads in 100 grams of fig paste, and 34 fruit fly eggs in every 8-ounce portion of golden raisins.

How do I know all this? Simple: I requested a copy of *Food Defect Action Levels* from the FDA's Center for Food Safety and Applied Nutrition. All the information is there in black and white in this nifty report's many tables and graphs. But don't get me wrong: I'm not shocked by this data. From a bug eater's standpoint, I'm happy to be getting more vitamins, minerals, and protein from so many of my store-bought staples.

About the Recipes

Theoretically, any dish with a food arthropod in it qualifies as eat-a-bug cuisine, but this doesn't mean you should just throw insects into your everyday fare. As in any recipe, the bugs must serve a purpose—by satisfying our appetites, adding a flavor or texture, or enhancing the visual appeal (or, I must admit, shock appeal) of a dish. Recipes for bug-based fare must also be artfully concocted so that the once-living ingredients can bring their special gifts to the table, ensuring a memorable (and I mean this in a positive way) meal.

Many of the recipes in this book were inspired by the culinary traditions of entomophagous societies—the Dayak of northern Borneo, the Yanomamo of Brazil, the South African Pedi, and the Shoshone of Wyoming, to name just a few. Several other recipes can be traced to less esoteric but almost as exotic sources, such as the restaurant La Cava del León in Sonora, Mexico, and the pharmaceutical shops of Vancouver's Chinatown. One

recipe is from the New York Entomological Society's Centennial Banquet, undoubtedly the most lavish insect-eating affair in the history of the Western world. A bunch of dishes (among them Three Bee Salad and Pest-o) have sprung from my overly fertile imagination or originated as bad puns.

I prefer to give top billing to the insect ingredients in my recipes, unlike some arthropod chefs who try to conceal the bugs in their dishes. Their recipes usually involve grinding the bodies of oven-dried crickets or mealworms into flour to be mixed with other, less controversial ingredients.

The bugs in my recipes look good: they are visual as well as gastronomic delights. Most are brightly colored and handsomely proportioned (a few are downright fetching), so why hide them or—worse—bury them beneath familiar foods? It's much better, I find, to prominently feature the bugs, artfully placing them atop a main dish or floating them on the surface of a tureen of soup. Do you think Martha Stewart would approve of my use of bug bodies and parts, along with forest greenery and fresh flowers, as garnishes? Presentation is everything, as they say.

This edition of my cookbook also contains new recipes generously contributed by four prominent bug eaters: Meeru Dhalwala, Dave Gracer, Zack Lemann, and Daniella Martin. All four of these chefs have freely shared their scientific knowledge and culinary tricks of the trade. I've competed in bug cook-offs with three of them in the past, and I have grown to respect their prowess and perspectives. I've included brief profiles of each of them in the introductions to their recipes.

Of course, dining on dragonflies is hardly the same as digging into a T-bone steak. Dishes featuring food arthropods fall under the heading of nouvelle cuisine, defined in my handy *Food Lover's Companion* as "fresher, lighter food served in small portions." Entrées such as Giant Water Bug on Watercress should not be served alone; rather, each main dish should be accompanied (or preceded) by an assortment of salads and side dishes, some with bugs and others without, to round out the mealtime experience and cleanse the palate.

Say No to Raw Bugs

Don't eat raw bugs. Like all other animals, insects and other land arthropods may carry parasites such as nematodes and roundworms, which can be passed on to warm-blooded animals, including people.

One way to kill harmful adult parasites is to freeze your ingredients. However, the parasites' eggs and intermediate forms may survive the freezing process, allowing the parasites to cause problems as they mature. Applying an external source of high heat (you know, cooking) is the only way to get these guys.

That's why the instructors at wilderness survival schools teach their students to roast all bugs and slugs in the flame of a candle, match, or cigarette lighter before popping them into their mouths. In this fashion, a U.S. Air Force fighter pilot, shot down behind enemy lines in Bosnia, survived on a diet of ants, leaves, and beetles lightly toasted with a cigarette lighter.

The Live Ingredients

Most of the bugs I've used in the following recipes are easy to purchase from a pet shop or biological supply company or, gather from the outdoors, seasonally, if not year-round. It's beyond the scope of this book to provide instruction in all aspects of arthropod acquisition. Entire volumes have been devoted to this subject, and detailed advice on collecting insects can be found in many introductory entomology texts, several of which are cited at the end of this book. Whenever possible, however, I've offered tips on catching the ingredients yourself.

Populations of insects and other land arthropods may be abundant, but they are not infinite. Most countries have not established limits to prevent collectors from exhausting land invertebrate resources, so everyone— including bug eaters—must exercise self-control. Otherwise it's way too easy to tip the ecological scales, upsetting a natural balance that has taken many millions of years to achieve.

While gathering ingredients for my dishes, I try to follow what is known among botanists as the one-in-twenty rule. I'll take an arthropod only if I am confident there are at least twenty of the same type nearby. This has never posed a problem with swarming species, where populations are often estimated in the billions, but it has limited my harvesting of many predatory arthropods—scorpions, for instance, which are never as abundant as their invertebrate prey. After reading *The Forgotten Pollinators* by Stephen Buchmann and Gary Nabhan, a sobering look at the rapid disappearance of the animal aides in the propagation of flowering plants, I've stopped harvesting moth and butterfly pupae and caterpillars from the wild. As Buchmann and Nabham point out, bees aren't the only insects that pollinate our food crops and ornamentals; the number of night-blooming plants would decline without help from moths, and butterflies are no less important in maintaining the diversity of our sun-loving flowers. Recognizing the importance of moths and butterflies to the environment, I've decided that only the larvae of pest species (such as clothes moths) or captive-reared ones (such as saturniid moths) are fair game in my book.

Many pet stores now carry live mealworms (the larvae of the darkling beetle, *Tenebrio*), wax worms, and house crickets as food for lizards and other vertebrates. These creatures are also available by mail from commercial suppliers of food insects and invertebrates for laboratory or classroom research. From these sources I've purchased termites, cockroaches, giant centipedes, and even Texas brown tarantulas. The names and addresses of my favorite livestock dealers are contained in this book's resources section.

Seasonal Availability of Edible Arthropods

	Jan	Feb	Mar	Apr	May	Jun	Jul	Aug	Sep	Oct	Nov	Dec
Grasshoppers				■	■	■	■	■	■			
Katydids				■	■	■	■	■	■			
Tomato Hornworms				■	■	■	■					
Giant Water Bugs			■	■	■	■	■	■	■	■	■	■
Saturniid Moth pupae	■	■	■						■	■	■	■
Termites												
winged queens							■	■				
workers and soldiers	■	■	■	■	■	■	■	■	■	■	■	■
Ants	■	■	■	■	■	■	■	■	■	■	■	■
Crickets	■	■	■	■	■	■	■	■	■	■	■	■
Cockroaches	■	■	■	■	■	■	■	■	■	■	■	■
Scorpions	■	■	■	■	■	■	■	■	■	■	■	■
Mealworms	■	■	■	■	■	■	■	■	■	■	■	■
Wax Moth larvae	■	■	■	■	■	■	■	■	■	■	■	■
Sow bugs	■	■	■	■	■	■	■	■	■	■	■	■

Cooking Techniques

Insects, spiders, and other land-dwelling arthropods are as quick and easy to cook as they are to acquire. In this book I've intentionally kept the food preparation techniques as straightforward as possible. Let's face it: working with stinging insects, biting spiders, and venomous scorpions, alive or dead, can test the mettle of most chefs, so why complicate things with elaborate procedures that distract one from the matters at hand?

If you've ever boiled a lobster, sautéed a scallop, or baked a package of frozen breaded shrimp, you should be able to master the cooking techniques in this book. There are no fancy tricks or elaborate preparations here—just an assortment of time-honored techniques for enjoying edible bugs.

Steaming is certainly the easiest way to cook arthropods. Some of these tasty critters, however, are too small for this technique. The bodies of termites, for instance, are tiny enough to fall through the holes in the bottom of a bamboo steamer.

Boiling is as uncomplicated as steaming, but with one drawback: while floating in their lightly salted bath, boiled arthropods can lose their already subtle flavor.

Sautéing is also a snap. The bite-sized bodies of many insects are suitably proportioned for a skillet or sauté pan. However, their small size (or, more accurately, their high surface-to-volume ratio) makes it easy to overcook them. Use medium heat and a wooden spoon

or metal spatula to turn the bugs so that they cook uniformly.

Stir-frying arthropods goes way back, to the dawn of Chinese civilization. A wok is ideal for cooking at high temperatures, allowing you to sear the exoskeleton and seal in much of the flavor. As this method's name implies, rapid stirring is required, as a wok's heat can vaporize the inner fluids of certain bugs (especially grubs and caterpillars), causing their bodies to swell and burst like balloons. That's a good reason to wear an apron when cooking these critters.

Deep-frying involves coating a bug in breadcrumbs or batter and is one way to make food arthropods more visually appealing. Dropping the coated bugs into a deep, heavy frying pan or wok, one-third to half full of oil, makes them taste better, too. Over the years, I've grown rather fond of my Fry Daddy Deep Fryer.

Dry-roasting arthropods is a widely practiced technique, the products of which can be added to many recipes, livening up even the most uninspired nonbug dishes.

Grilling with the modern equivalent of the old-fashioned fire pit (a wood, gas, or electric barbecue) is particularly appropriate for certain large-bodied insects and their kin.

Choice Cuts

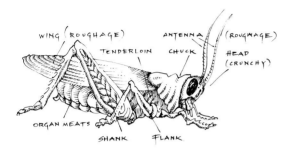

There's not a lot of what we think of as "meat" on most food arthropods. The large strands of longitudinal muscle (the dark meat, so to speak) that operate an arthropod's legs, wings, and tail are sumptuous fare, whether they happen to belong to a scorpion or a snow crab. Unlike with chickens or turkeys, the masses of transverse muscle (the white meat) are at a premium, usually contained in the fleshy tail and body segments.

The thoraxes and abdomens of arthropods are filled with organ meats. No, this doesn't mean that the meal is accompanied by music, nor should diners expect servings of liver and onions or kidney pie. Arthropods don't have hearts, kidneys, brains, or lungs as we generally think of them. Instead, these creatures depend on such things as Malpighian tubules (the squiggly little excretory organs of insects) or book

lungs (paired respiratory organs with pagelike lamellae, unique to spiders and their kin).

In most insects, particularly the plant-eating ones, the largest organs are devoted to digestion. A huge expandable sac, the crop, stores freshly chomped food. The gizzard grinds the food, and the stomach (which monopolizes most of the interior space) removes nutrients from the food. Since it can take several days for an arthropod to digest its food, there's a good chance your meal will be flavored by whatever the bug ate last.

Much of an arthropod's bulk is tied up in its exoskeleton—a fact confirmed by the wrecking-yard's-worth of spare body parts littering one's plate at an all-you-can-eat crab feast. This exoskeleton is made up of chitin, a material that scientists know as N-acetylglucosamine, a polysaccharide interwoven with fibrous proteins. We bug eaters know chitin as the stuff that, like the husks of popcorn kernels, invariably wedges itself in the gaps between our teeth.

Some warm-blooded animals, including lemurs and insectivorous bats, produce an enzyme that breaks down chitin during digestion. Human digestive juices contain only small stocks of this enzyme, primarily as a defense against parasites and tiny, hard-bodied critters like dust mites. So aside from roughage, we derive little, if any, benefit from eating an arthropod's chitinous skin. Incidentally, the same can be said about the skin of an apple. However, since most recipes call for food arthropods with their skin on, diners must learn to gracefully transfer any crunched chitin to the side of a soup bowl or salad plate. Hosts can make things easier by providing a separate receptacle (similar to the communal dish for mussel shells and shrimp peels at a paella feast) for this purpose.

Growing Your Own Bugs

Today's emphasis on food security, or the ability of all people to access adequate supplies of nutritious food at all times, has inspired many of us to create mini-livestock farms where we can breed and rear sufficient quantities of bugs to feed our friends and families. Mini-farming makes sense in economic terms, too: the cost of shipping live crickets and other goodies can often exceed that of the critters themselves.

For these reasons I encourage you to consider raising your own mealworms and wax worms. Such an endeavor is surprisingly easy, even in a studio apartment, and I've seen several designs for stackable rearing trays that can easily fit in an armoire or a kitchen cabinet.

A basic mealworm farm begins with the acquisition of three plastic sweater storage boxes—you know, the ones designed to slide under a bed. Drill air holes in the lids of the boxes and fill the bottoms of two of them with a three- or four-inch layer of uncooked whole-grain oatmeal. In the third box, put a one-inch layer of oatmeal. The oatmeal serves as a bedding material in which the mealworms will grow and develop before transforming themselves into adult darkling beetles. Next add seventy-five to a hundred starter mealworms to each of the first two containers. For moisture, add a small wedge of cabbage, an orange slice, or half a potato. You can augment this with a wet sponge in an open container that rests on top of the oats. Change the fruit or vegetable scraps weekly, letting a few days pass with no food in the boxes before replacing it, which helps prevent mildew or mold from growing.

Every few days gently comb through the colony. Discard any dead mealworms and put the live pupae in the third container. The pupae will mature in about three weeks, give or take a few days. Now you'll have plenty of adults to bring in the next generation of mini-farm stock.

Don't expect rapid results. Depending on what they are fed and the temperature in your house, it can take about one hundred to two hundred days for your starter mealworms to complete their life cycle. I've been told that if you intend to harvest mealworms in the spring, you'll need to start your colony in late fall or early winter. And don't be discouraged: the mealworm eggs and hatchlings are barely visible to the unaided eye, but after a few weeks you should start seeing the youngsters gliding beneath the surface of the bran.

Wax worms are nearly as easy to raise in your home. The University of Kentucky College of Agriculture offers good advice on doing this, available as a fact sheet that can be downloaded from their website, www.ca.uky.edu/entomology/entfacts/ef011.asp.

Crickets and grasshoppers are susceptible to viruses and other diseases, making these little beasts considerably more difficult to rear, regardless of the scale of the operation.

Beware of Bad Bugs

Not every bug is fit to be eaten. Fortunately for us, the inedible ones are cunning enough to tell us so. Brightly hued insects—especially those wearing spots or stripes of red, yellow, or orange—may look nifty, but these loud colors are really signals to back off. This is how bugs announce their unpalatability, warning other animals away from these walking examples of bad taste.

A few vibrant-hued insects are actually imposters, disguising themselves to capitalize on the distasteful reputations of other species. The technical term for such duplicity (should you seek to impress your friends) is Batesian mimicry. The Batesian look-alikes might taste fine, but unless you really know your bugs, it's better to read the signs and steer clear.

Bees, wasps, scorpions, some spiders, and certain insects can bite or sting those trying to cook or eat them. In most instances, the pain from being punctured dissipates within an hour or two, but on rare occasions more concerted care may be needed. Erring on the side of caution, I highly recommend that chefs work only with frozen and thawed specimens. Even if you're working with a dead scorpion, though, you can still pierce a finger on the animal's stinger. This is also true of large tarantulas,

which have scimitar-sharp recurved fangs. For this reason I always begin by disarming my dangerous bugs using an X-Acto blade or paring knife, removing any organic weaponry and the associated venom glands.

Eating bugs may trigger allergic reactions in a small percentage of diners, often but not always in the same people who are allergic to crab, lobster, or shrimp. Symptoms can range from a rash or runny nose to labored breathing or, in severe instances, shock. So if you know you're allergic to shellfish, please stay away from edible bugs. And if you *do* have an allergic reaction to any bug-based meal, consult your physician immediately—even if it feels like you're making a big deal out of a little bug.

The Best Beverages for Bugs

I'd be remiss if I failed to suggest a selection of wines to sip with eat-a-bug entrées and sides. Although there are few rules about such pairings, one need only turn to the sea-dwelling cousins of land arthropods, the crustaceans, for guidelines. After all, many of the bugs in my recipes taste like lobster or crab.

Already celebrated in the Pacific Northwest as *the* wine to pair with seafood, Pinot Gris is a fine companion for bug cuisine. With its light body and restrained flavor, it enhances the subtle taste of stir-fried dragonflies and other daintily seasoned Asian dishes.

Equally acclaimed among seafood connoisseurs is Sauvignon Blanc. This grape variety produces wines with a crisp acidity and, in some vintages, a fruitiness that complements the woodsy taste of field crickets or other wild-caught fare.

Joe Euro, the proprietor of my favorite wine shop, turned me on to a selection of sparkling wines that work well with arthropods. Among his favorites are the tasty sparklers made by Scharffenberger and Iron Horse in Northern California and an Italian Prosecco made by Rotari. "Let's not overlook champagne," he says. "There's nothing better than some bubbly to wash down bugs."

The robust flavors of a few arthropod dishes (grilled centipedes, for instance, as prepared on page 106) may warrant stronger stuff. A pitcher of sangria or a six-pack of Heineken beer may be appropriate on these occasions. When considering a red wine, I recommend a medium-bodied Zinfandel or a Pinot Noir. Stay away from heavyweights such as Cabernet, which can overwhelm a meal of insects.

" Red, orange, or yellow—forgo this small fellow. Black, green or brown—go ahead and toss him down.**"** —DGG

PART ONE

DON'T WORRY, BE HOPPY

Nine Culinary Leaps of Faith, Using
Crickets, Grasshoppers, and Their Kin

> **"** Say *L'Chaim*, 'To life,' the next time you bite into a migratory locust or any of its kosher kin. **"** —DGG

There are about twenty thousand species in the order Orthoptera, which, in the words of my favorite know-it-all, the nineteenth-century naturalist Reverend J. G. Wood, contains "some of the finest and, at the same time, the most grotesquely formed members of the insect tribe."

During Reverend Wood's time, cockroaches, praying mantises, and stick insects were regarded as card-carrying orthopterans. Today, however, membership has been restricted to crickets, grasshoppers, locusts, and katydids. These animals are easily recognized by their narrow leathery forewings; broad, membranous hind wings; and muscular hind legs that are well developed for jumping. Of course, there are exceptions, even among this select clan. For example, the mole cricket—a small brown-bodied burrowing plant pest—more closely resembles a crayfish than Cousin Jiminy.

In some parts of the world, Orthoptera are sources of entertainment as well as food—live dinner theater, if you will. In Japan, for instance, singing katydids and crickets are kept as pets, confined in miniature cages with slender bamboo bars. Throughout China, the sport of cricket fighting is guaranteed to draw sizable crowds, with betting far livelier than at horse races or kickboxing events.

Orthoptera are relished by the indigenous people of Africa, Australia, South and Central America, Mexico, the Middle East, and many Pacific islands. Even in the largely unentomophagous United States, there's been some interest in orthopteran edibles. Many of us fondly remember chocolate-covered grasshoppers, sold in tins by Reese Finer Foods in the early 1960s. Although these particular treats are no longer commercially available, one can still purchase chocolate-covered crickets from Hotlix of Pismo Beach, California, which makes Cricket Lick-It lollipops and other insect-oriented novelty foods.

FOOD FOR THOUGHT

- Like big words? Then you'll love "saltatorial," defined by *Webster's New Collegiate Dictionary* as "relating to, marked by, or adapted for leaping (as in the legs of a grasshopper)."
- Research conducted in Jerusalem confirms that uncooked desert locusts are good for you, composed of 75 percent protein, 3.4 percent fat, and 7.5 percent carbohydrates and chock-full of iron, calcium, sulfur, riboflavin, and niacin.
- If humans had the athletic abilities of either grasshoppers or crickets, the entrants in the Olympic Games could easily break all existing records, clearing the high jump bar at three hundred feet and exceeding five hundred feet in the broad jump competition.
- Bas-reliefs dating back to 700 B.C.E. show the servants of the Assyrian king Sennacherib bearing locusts skewered on sticks in preparation for a feast.
- Jiminy Cricket won an Oscar for his rendition of "When You Wish Upon a Star" in the Disney film *Pinocchio*.

One of the largest insect-rearing operations in the western hemisphere, Fluker Farms of Port Allen, Louisiana, sells more than three million house crickets (*Acheta domesticus*) in a week. Admittedly, most of these are sold as bait for sport fishing and food for pet reptiles and amphibians. Still, a small percentage of the company's stock is destined for human consumption, primarily at zoo- or museum-sponsored events. Fluker's clients include at least one restaurant, Typhoon, a pan-Asian eatery at the Santa Monica Airport in California, which features crickets in its Taiwanese stir-fry dishes. An appetizer portion is about six ounces before frying, says Typhoon's proprietor, Brian Vidor. "We really don't know what the crickets weigh," he jokes, "because they hop off the scale too quickly."

Locusts in Leviticus

Nearly all the Orthoptera are vegetarians, favoring fresh leaves and stems and forgoing any plant (or animal) matter that's decayed. This dietary preference, which is innately more hygienic than scavenging, may explain why locusts were determined to be kosher (that is, fit for human consumption) in the Old Testament.

In Leviticus, the book of the Bible in which the dietary laws are first addressed, the text plainly states that "all winged insects that go upon all fours are an abomination to you." But despite this seemingly hard line against bug eating, a few entomophagous alternatives are identified. "These you may eat; the *arbeh* after his kind, the *sal'am* after his kind, the *chargol* after his kind, and the *chagav* after his kind."

Most entomologists agree that *arbeh*, *sal'am*, *chargol*, and *chagav* are just different names for the same critter, the locust, in various stages of development. Some suggest that locusts were included in the list of kosher foods because they are so easily distinguished from other insects, thus limiting the chances of the devout mistakenly snacking on a species deemed impure.

Beating the Bush for Big Bugs

Orthoptera, not bison, was the seasonal mainstay of many Plains tribes. Harvesting the abundant stocks was often a communal effort, with entire villages—men, women, and children—working together to flush the six-legged game.

"They begin by digging a hole, ten or twelve feet in diameter, by four or five deep," wrote Father Pierre-Jean De Smet, describing the tactics of the Shoshone in the 1800s:

> Then, armed with long branches of artemisia, they surround a field of four or five acres, more or less, according to the number of people who are engaged in it. They stand about twenty feet apart and their whole work is to beat the ground, so as to frighten up the grasshoppers and make them bound forward. They chase them toward the center by degrees—that is, into the hole prepared for their reception. Their number is so considerable that frequently three or four acres furnish grasshoppers sufficient to fill the reservoir or hole.

This orthopteran bounty could be hastily handpicked and stuffed into sacks, which were then soaked in saltwater and—how convenient—tossed into an oven for ten or fifteen minutes. Other tribes built large fires in their insect-catching pits, creating a bed of coals on which to roast any grasshoppers headed that way. Some tribes simply torched the grasslands and returned once the fires had died down to pluck the flame-broiled insects straight from the scorched earth and eat them.

The potential of the various harvest techniques was nicely illustrated by entomologist David Madsen, who, with the help of a few peers, rounded up Mormon crickets (*Anabrus simplex*) along the Utah-Colorado border. Two sweeps of the underbrush brought in batches of 5,652 and 9,876 crickets, for an average catch of nearly eighteen and a half pounds. A pound of dried Mormon crickets contains about 1,270 calories, so the nutritional rewards from such a catch were quite large. In one hour Madsen's team had amassed the caloric equivalent of forty-three Big Macs, forty-nine slices of pizza, or eighty-nine chili dogs.

Travels with My Ant: A Debut Gone Awry

A week after the release of the original *Eat-a-Bug Cookbook* in 1998, I was invited to appear on *Late Night with Conan O'Brien*, the quirkiest of TV talk shows at the time.

I flew from Seattle to New York, eager to make my debut on network TV. Conan's segment producer greeted me backstage. It had been his life's ambition to get Conan to eat a cockroach on TV he told me.

"No problem," I said. In my carry-on luggage I'd packed a dozen baked and seasoned cockroaches, complete with cellophane-tipped toothpicks. I'd also brought scorpions, crickets, and dried ants—all the fixings for a real feast.

O'Brien was a trooper, milking every moment of our interview for all it was worth. He called me a freak during my segment's introduction and asked me if I was offended when he referred to the ingredients in my dishes as "vermin." But he did eat a bug—one of the cockroaches, lightly dusted with Tony Chachere's seasoning mix.

The producer met me in the wings after the segment. He gave me an autographed photo of Conan and a T-shirt from the show before escorting me to the street, where an airport limo awaited.

Several months later I called Conan's producer to ask him if he'd consider having me back on his show. I proposed doing a special Martha Stewart-esque Thanksgiving segment, during which I'd unveil an assortment of seasonal delights, culminating, of course, with my granny's recipe for Cranberry Cockroach Relish.

That's when I learned about Conan's deep-seated fear of insects. Even at 6 feet 4 inches, the redheaded host of America's favorite late-night TV show didn't want to be anywhere near the tiny six-legged ingredients in my dishes. It was sad but true, the producer explained, that the show's host had let his uneasiness get the best of him, and he had become ill shortly after I had left the building.

"I'd like to invite you back, but I don't think Conan will go for it," the producer explained, ending our chat.

CHAPTER 1

COOKING WITH CRICKETS

> **"**Oh cricket, from your cheery cry; No one would ever guess; How quickly you must die.**"**
> —Matsuo Bashō (1644–94)

Gryllus, the scientific name for the field cricket, is an open invitation to catch this insect and cook it. So is the delightfully optimistic chirp produced by this creature and its first cousin, the European house cricket.

The cricket's reputation as a songster has been celebrated by John Milton ("Far from all resort of mirth, Save the cricket on the hearth") and Charles Dickens ("I have loved it for the many times I've heard it and the many thoughts its harmless music has given me"). Although I cook exclusively with crickets that have been frozen and thawed, I still like to keep a few live crickets on hand at all times, just so that they can serenade my guests and me.

Where crickets are especially abundant, edible specimens can be most efficiently captured by taking broad, upward swipes at tall grass or shrubbery with a short-handled net. Entomologists call this technique "sweeping." A more leisurely approach involves the setting of what are commonly known as pitfall traps.

Here's how it works: Dig a small hole with a garden trowel and sink a quart mason jar so the top is flush with the surface of the ground. Cover the mouth of the jar with a piece of wood that is held half an inch above the ground by pebbles or twigs. Crickets that walk under the wood and into the trap will be unable to hop out and must stay there until you retrieve them.

Store-bought crickets are more appealing to lazy-bugs like me. They're also more environmentally friendly: there's no reason to worry about overharvesting, as these tasty morsels have been

ENTO-EPHEMERA

The word "cricket" comes from the French *criquet*, which means "little creaker." However, only adult male crickets make noise. To do this, they rub their wings together. The friction causes the cricket's wings to vibrate at a rate of as many as five thousand times a second. The vibrations reach our ears as shrill chirps, which can be heard from a distance of nearly a mile.

bred in large quantities for the sole purpose of being eaten. Many pet stores now carry live house crickets as food for hedgehogs, bearded dragons, frogs, and other household insectivores.

Crickets can also be ordered directly from livestock suppliers, although these businesses may require that you purchase as many as a thousand crickets at a time. Don't worry if a livestock supplier is your only option; the extra crickets can be frozen and stored for later use.

Both captured and commercially reared live crickets should be kept in an empty ten-gallon aquarium or plastic storage bin. Either container must have a tight-fitting top, preferably made of fine mesh or perforated with small holes to ensure adequate ventilation. A light sprinkling of oatmeal makes a nice floor covering, and a stack of inverted cardboard egg cartons creates a series of dark recesses and chambers through which the crickets can creep. Place a moistened sponge in one corner of the tank and a few pieces of wilted lettuce in another corner. You've now created the cricket equivalent of Club Med.

Be forewarned that adult male crickets are territorial. They will aggressively defend their turf—a trait that, under crowded conditions, is sure to cause trouble in paradise. Inspect your cricket colony each day for fatalities, removing any losers of the to-the-death contests.

Once the time comes to harvest your crickets, scoop up the desired number of live individuals. Be quick about it: these fellas can really jump! Transfer the crickets to a smaller container, also with a tight-fitting lid (a plastic cottage cheese carton with a perforated top is a worthy vessel), and put the container in the freezer. After an hour or two, when the crickets are frozen solid, they can be stored en masse in plastic freezer bags. When you are ready to use them, they can be poured into a colander, rinsed with cold water, and employed in a number of dishes.

CRICKET-COOKING TIPS

When purchasing crickets, ask for sixth or seventh instars, which are three- or four-week-old nymphs, just a molt or two away from attaining adulthood. These nymphs lack the chitinous wings of adults, so they are less crunchy.

Their relatively large surface-to-volume ratio means that crickets are easily overcooked. When sautéing or stir-frying use moderate heat and turn the crickets frequently with a wooden spoon or other utensil.

The weight-conscious might want to know that one cup of crickets (about 8 ounces) contains approximately 250 calories and 6 grams of fat.

NIBLETS AND CRICKLETS

Yield: 6 servings

Since I am often on the road, equipped with nothing but my single-burner hotplate, a Fry Daddy, and a suitcase full of cooking supplies, I've had to devise a pared-down alternative to what *Time* magazine has called my signature dish, Orthopteran Orzo. The following recipe is undeniably low-tech. Heck, if you buy water chestnuts and yellow corn in those fancy pop-top cans, you won't even need a can opener.

Although it is easier to make, this dish is no less nutritious than its fancier counterpart. Like Orthopteran Orzo, it's nutritionally balanced, with carbohydrates and protein in their recommended ratios, and it takes minutes, not hours, to prepare. Although I use butter at home, I prefer margarine, which doesn't burn as easily, when I'm cooking for TV crews or in unfamiliar settings.

2 tablespoons butter or margarine

$^1/_2$ cup chopped yellow onion

1 cup frozen 6-week-old (adult) crickets, thawed

$^1/_2$ cup canned sliced water chestnuts, diced

1 cup canned yellow corn, drained and liquid reserved

2 tablespoons chopped fresh basil

2 teaspoons garlic powder

Salt and freshly ground pepper to taste

1. In a wok or large skillet, melt the butter over medium heat. Add the chopped onions and cook, stirring, until they have softened. Now add the crickets and sauté for about 3 minutes.

2. Add the water chestnuts and corn. Stir in 1 or 2 tablespoons of the reserved liquid from the corn.

3. Stir in the basil and garlic powder and season with salt and pepper to taste. Reduce the heat to low, cook for 1 minute more, and serve. Goodness—that *was* quick and easy, wasn't it?

ORTHOPTERAN ORZO

Yield: 6 servings

Orzo, a rice-shaped pasta, gets its name from the Italian word for barley, but we all know that orzo looks exactly like juvenile bugs. Needless to say, it's a perfect complement for crickets, especially three- or four-week-old nymphs, which are of a comparable size. At this stage in life the young crickets lack wings and ovipositors, the chitinous tubes through which the adult females pass their eggs. Their limbs are skinny, so there's no need to remove them before cooking. Likewise for the antennae, which, at less than a quarter of an inch, should pose no obstacle to enjoying this meal.

3 cups vegetable broth

1 cup orzo

$^1/_2$ cup grated carrot

$^1/_4$ cup finely diced red bell pepper

$^1/_4$ cup finely diced green bell pepper

1 tablespoon butter

1 clove garlic, minced

$^1/_2$ cup chopped yellow onion

1 cup frozen two- or three-week-old cricket nymphs, thawed

2 tablespoons chopped fresh parsley

1. Bring the broth to a boil, then stir in the orzo.

2. Continue boiling the orzo until it is tender, about 10 minutes; drain any extra liquid, then quickly add the carrot and red and green peppers. Mix evenly and set aside.

3. In a separate skillet, melt the butter and add the garlic, onion, and crickets. Sauté briefly until the onions are translucent and the garlic and crickets have browned.

4. Combine the cricket mixture, including any liquid, with the orzo and vegetables, top with the parsley, and serve.

CHIRPY CHEX PARTY MIX

Yield: 6 servings

I gained valuable insights about both crickets and Cajun cuisine from Zack Lemann, the manager of Animal and Visitor Programs at the Audubon Butterfly Garden and Insectarium in New Orleans. I met Zack in June 1997 at the first annual Bug Banquet, a gala affair at the Louisiana Nature Center. There he was merrily greeting the public, doling out free samples of Mushrooms and Mealworms, Cricket Fritters, and (please, don't even ask) Toffee Surprise. I've included Zack's prize-winning recipe for Odonate Hors d'Oeuvres, pan-fried dragonflies served on slices of portobello mushroom, on page 112.

All the dishes served that hot summer day were exceptionally well prepared. However, it was the fire in Zack's Crispy Cajun Crickets that really warmed my heart. The secret ingredient to this flavorful creation, I later learned, is Tony Chachere's Creole Seasoning, a down-home product from Opelousas, Louisiana, that is "Great on Everything!" just like its label proclaims.

To prepare his zesty cricket dish, Zack first melts butter in a skillet. Then he tosses in a fistful of dry-roasted crickets, blasting them with the capsaicin-rich Tony Chachere's, and gently stirs the crickets until they are cooked through. Before transferring them to a serving bowl he dusts them with more of the Creole seasoning mix.

"Don't be bashful," Zack says. "There's no such thing as too much Tony's. People in New Orleans practically live on this stuff."

Zack's formula for pan-fried Crispy Cajun Crickets inspired this recipe for Chirpy Chex Party Mix. If you can't find Tony Chachere's on the shelves of your local grocery, you'll have to get by with the traditional Chex mix seasonings plus a bit of chile powder for heat. For the $1/4$ cup of Tony Chachere's in this recipe, substitute 1 tablespoon Lawry's Seasoned Salt, 2 teaspoons garlic powder, 2 teaspoons onion powder, 1 teaspoon freshly ground black pepper, and $1/2$ teaspoon New Mexico chile powder.

6 tablespoons butter or margarine

2 tablespoons Worcestershire sauce

$1/_4$ cup Tony Chachere's Creole Seasoning, plus extra for dusting

8 cups assorted Chex cereals (corn, wheat, and rice) or other dry, unsweetened cereals

2 cups Crispy Crickets (recipe follows)

1 cup pretzels

1 cup dry-roasted Spanish peanuts

1. Preheat the oven to 250°F.

2. In a roasting pan on the stovetop over medium heat, melt the butter. Stir in the Worcestershire sauce and creole seasoning.

3. Add the cereals, crickets, pretzels, and peanuts and stir until each piece is coated evenly with seasoning mixture.

4. Bake in the oven for 1 hour, stirring every 15 minutes.

5. Pour the mixture into a brown paper bag, dust liberally with more creole seasoning, and shake. Let cool to room temperature before serving.

Crispy Crickets

1. Preheat the oven to 225°F. Spread 1 cup of clean, frozen crickets (250 adults or 1,500 4-week-old nymphs) evenly on a lightly oiled baking sheet. The actual cricket count may vary, depending on the life stage of the specimens being used, but for the best results, use crickets that are all roughly the same size.

2. Bake until crickets are crisp, around 20 minutes.

3. If you'd like to remove the crickets' legs, antennae, and ovipositors, put the baked crickets in a clean brown paper bag. Shake the bag vigorously and many of these throat-tickling bits will break off, enabling you to separate the wheat from the chaff, so to speak.

CRICKET SEASONING À LA VIJ'S

Yield: $1/2$ cup

In 2010, with some initial coaching from me, Meeru Dhalwala and her husband Vikram Vij, co-owners of Vij's, a renowned Indian restaurant in Vancouver, British Columbia, created the recipe for what they eventually named Cricket Paratha. For this dish they seasoned crickets with Indian spices and roasted them before grinding them into a powder, blending it with chapati flour, and baking the results. Stuffed with onion, turnips, and other savory ingredients, the flatbread was cut into small triangles and served as an appetizer to Vij's clientele. The dish was an immediate hit. "We know we're on to something if we can get our customers to enjoy a dish with both crickets *and* turnips," Vikram told me with a grin.

Meeru was reluctant to share her paratha recipe with me—she says the steps for making good Indian flatbreads are too involved to be easily communicated in print—but she gave me her recipe for the seasoning mix that she sprinkles on her Spicy Roasted Crickets, one of nearly a hundred dishes in her recent *Vij's at Home* cookbook.

Try this spice mixture in place of Tony Chachere's Creole Seasoning for some added zing to your next Chirpy Chex Party Mix (page 28). Meeru's exquisite spice mixture takes only 30 minutes to make, including the 20 minutes it takes to cool.

---

1 heaping teaspoon whole cloves

$1^1/_2$ teaspoons black cardamom seeds (from about 10 whole cardamom pods)

6 tablespoons whole cumin seeds

1 tablespoon pounded cinnamon sticks

$1/_4$ teaspoon ground mace (optional)

$1/_4$ teaspoon nutmeg

1. In a heavy frying pan over medium-high heat, combine the cloves, cardamom seeds, cumin seeds, and cinnamon sticks. Cook, stirring constantly, until the cumin seeds darken. Remove the pan from the heat and transfer the spices to a bowl. Allow to cool for 20 minutes.

2. Using a spice or coffee grinder or a mortar and pestle, combine the cooled toasted spices with the mace and nutmeg. Grind until the mixture has the consistency of store-bought ground black pepper.

3. Sprinkle liberally on defrosted crickets before baking them as instructed on page 29. Store any extra seasoning in an airtight container for future use.

BUGS IN A RUG

Yield: 6 servings

Ronald Taylor and Barbara Carter's Cricket Rumaki, a recipe that was published in their ground-breaking *Entertaining with Insects*, is the only orthopteran appetizer ever served to Johnny Carson, the host of the *Tonight Show* from the 1960s to the 1990s. Although the classic formula for rumaki (and Taylor and Carter's recipe for the tasty cricket treat) calls for water chestnuts, I've substituted pineapple chunks—a tip of the hat to my neighbors to the north, who frequently sprinkle this tropical fruit and Canadian bacon on top of their so-called "Hawaiian" pizzas. I've also upped the ante for this hot hors d'oeuvre by skewering two crickets on each toothpick, only one of which is truly "snug" in its lean bacon "rug."

$^1/_2$ cup olive oil

2 tablespoons champagne vinegar or other high-quality white wine vinegar

3 tablespoons chopped fresh mint or dill

2 cloves garlic, minced

24 frozen house crickets, thawed

12 chunks canned pineapple

6 slices very lean bacon

1. Combine the oil, vinegar, mint, and garlic in a bowl. Add the crickets and pineapple, cover the bowl, and refrigerate for 8 to 12 hours.

2. Preheat the broiler.

3. Cut each slice of bacon in half lengthwise, then into thirds.

4. Place one cricket on top of a pineapple chunk in a lifelike pose. Wrap a strip of bacon around both. Impale another cricket with a toothpick, gently pushing the cricket to the wide end of the pick. Pierce the bacon, cricket, and pineapple chunk with the toothpick to hold them together. Place the toothpick on a baking sheet and repeat with rest of toothpicks—12 in all.

5. Broil for several minutes on each side, or until the bacon is brown.

6. Serve hot.

CHOCOLATE CRICKET TORTE

Yield: 6 servings

The New York Entomological Society's Centennial Banquet may have been one of the ritziest and most extensively covered events in the history of bug eating. Held in 1992 at the headquarters of the Explorer's Club in Midtown Manhattan, this lavish affair was organized by Louis Sorkin, entomologist at the American Museum of Natural History. The banquet featured an array of tantalizing items, including Spiced Crickets and Mealworm Balls in Zesty Tomato Sauce.

"As a consciousness-raising event, the banquet was successful," admitted John Rennie, who filed his firsthand report in the August 1992 issue of *Scientific American* magazine. Rennie enjoyed the roasted crickets (which he found "almost indistinguishable from roasted peanuts") but was turned off by the Thai water bugs, deemed to be "too similar to giant cockroaches" in his view.

A year later the Centennial Banquet was reenacted for a Japanese television crew. This time the menu had a Far Eastern flair and featured such delicacies as Mealworm Nori Balls and Cricket Tempura with Apricot Dipping Sauce.

A memorable dessert at both banquets was the Chocolate Cricket Torte, reproduced here with the permission of Louis Sorkin. I've added chopped walnuts, which add texture to this already crunchy dessert.

1 cup (2 sticks) butter
2 ounces unsweetened chocolate
6 ounces semisweet chocolate
4 eggs, separated
$1/2$ cup sugar
$1/2$ cup strong brewed coffee
$1/2$ cup coarsely chopped walnuts
1 cup Crispy Crickets (page 29), coarsely chopped

1. Preheat the oven to 350°F. Butter the inside of an 8-inch springform pan and dust it lightly with flour.

2. In the top of a double boiler, melt both the chocolates with the butter, stirring frequently, until melted. Set aside and allow to cool to room temperature.

3. In a bowl, whisk together the egg yolks, sugar, and coffee. Add the cooled chocolate mixture, chopped walnuts, and Crispy Crickets to the bowl and stir to combine.

4. In a separate clean bowl, whip the egg whites until they stand in soft peaks. Stir the egg whites gently into the chocolate mixture.

5. Bake until the torte is set but the center is still moist, 30 to 40 minutes. Allow the torte to cool for 10 minutes before removing from pan.

CHAPTER 2

GRILLED GRASSHOPPERS, CREAMED KATYDIDS, AND LOCUSTS LOVINGLY PREPARED

❝ Before Copulation the Males are of the more delicate taste, afterwards the Females, for that they have in them white eggs very pleasant to the palat[e]. **❞**
—Thomas Mouffet on grasshoppers, in *The Theater of Insects* (1658)

Grasshoppers are basically giant crickets with large, powerful hind legs and big but streamlined bodies. The carcass of the eastern lubber (*Romalea guttata*), North America's largest grasshopper species, can exceed three inches. That's pretty big by bug standards.

Katydids belong to the long-horned grasshopper family, Tettigoniidae. They can be identified by their lovely antennae, which extend in a graceful arc well beyond the folded wingtips and the long, swordlike ovipositors (egg-laying tubes) of the adult animals. The bright green color of many katydids, which is a result of the foliage these animals eat, is an aid in concealment.

Locusts are little more than grasshoppers with large wings that migrate in swarms. But let's not downplay their impact on the environment. Remember that locust swarms were among the ten plagues directed at the Egyptians by Moses, inspiring them to set his people free. In 1875 an observer in Nebraska wrote of a locust swarm that was one hundred miles wide, three hundred miles long, and, in places, a tad short of a mile high. Estimating that each cubic yard contained twenty-seven locusts, he determined that nearly twenty-eight million flying grasshoppers were packed into each cubic mile of air space. From this figure, and the fact that the swarm remained this dense for six hours and moved at speeds of at least five miles an hour, he calculated that this particular swarm was comprised of more than 124 billion locusts—a number nearly eighteen times greater than the present-day population of humans.

"So assiduously do they apply their busy jaws that the peculiar sound produced by the champing of the leaves, twigs and grass blades can be heard at a considerable distance," observed the eloquent Reverend J. G. Wood, a nineteenth-century naturalist, in his *Illustrated Natural History*. "When they take to flight, the rushing of their wings is like the roaring of the sea; as their armies pass through the air, the sky is darkened as if by black thunder clouds."

In his book *Animate Creation*, Wood told of the Kalahari Bushman, one of the only individuals "who welcomes the Locust with all his heart." Such an individual, he wrote, "has no crops to lose, no clothing to be destroyed, and only sees in the swarming insects his greatest luxury, namely an abundant supply of food without any trouble in obtaining it."

HARVESTING HINT

You don't have to wait for a windfall such as a plague of locusts to harvest grasshoppers or katydids for your own culinary purposes. Both can be harvested from the wild, using either a sweep net by day or a widemouthed capture jar for handpicking at night. In Europe you can also purchase immature and adult farm-reared locusts at pet stores.

Although your catch can be housed in a similar fashion as crickets, many species are selective grazers, feeding only on certain plants. Without access to these, your livestock may perish after a few days or weeks. For this reason it's a good idea to keep any captured wild grasshoppers or katydids for only one or two days—just long enough for you to observe their behaviors and short enough for these animals to survive on their inner food reserves. After that they should be sent to the freezer—and the sleep from which no orthopteran ever awakens.

Inspired by the prospect of a free meal, the Kalahari Bushmen built large fires in the paths of locusts, and the insects, "being stifled with the smoke and having their wings scorched by the flames," would drop from on high, falling like rain on the desert's arid plain. Here they were gathered into heaps, roasted, and eaten whole. Leftovers were ground between two stones, producing a kind of meal that was then dried in the sun and "kept for a considerable period without becoming putrid," according to Wood.

" Locusts can also be dried and stored as a protein-rich powder. Here is one flavor not yet discovered by Howard Johnson or Baskin Robbins.**"** —Calvin W. Schwabe, *Unmentionable Cuisine*

CREAM OF KATYDID SOUP

Yield: 6 servings

My two favorite harbingers of springtime—fresh, organically grown asparagus at our local produce stand and the trills of insect choristers in the evening air—come together in this delicious dish.

When cooking in southern climes, I've always been enthralled by the ratchetlike voices of katydids emanating from the shrubbery. "Katy-did, katy-didn't, katy-did," these insects bicker for hours on end.

Living many hundreds of miles from the heart of katydid country (although the various katydid species are spread across North America, they seem to make their sonic presence best known in the southern United States), I was forced to purchase the live ingredients for the following chlorophyll-rich Cream of Katydid Soup from an online livestock supplier in Thibodaux, Louisiana. It was a costly buy, but it sure beat the airfare, hotel tab, and rental car expense to mount a katydid safari all by myself.

$^1/_4$ cup butter
1 clove garlic, minced
$^3/_4$ cup chopped yellow onion
14 frozen katydids, thawed
1 quart vegetable broth
24 to 28 spears (4 cups) asparagus
$^1/_2$ cup buttermilk or heavy cream
Salt and freshly ground pepper to taste

1. In a large pot over medium heat, melt the butter. Add the garlic and onions and sauté until they are soft and golden.

2. Add 8 of the katydids and the vegetable broth; bring to a boil.

3. Trim $^1/_2$ inch from the end of each asparagus spear and discard. Chop the spears into $^1/_2$-inch pieces. Set aside asparagus tips and drop the rest of the stalks into the boiling broth. Cover, reduce the heat to low, and simmer for 45 minutes.

4. Working in batches if necessary, carefully transfer the soup to a blender and purée.

5. Return the soup to pot, add the reserved asparagus tips, and simmer until they are tender, 5 to 10 minutes. Remove from heat and let cool

6. Stir in the buttermilk, season with salt and pepper to taste, cover, and chill.

7. Immediately before serving, float the remaining katydids on the surface of each bowl of soup for garnish. Tell your guests not to eat this insect. It's just there for appearance's sake.

OAXACAN WHOPPERS

Yield: 6 servings

In villages throughout the arid state of Oaxaca, Mexico, grasshoppers are boiled and then dried in the sun before being brought to the marketplace. There they are fried in lard; seasoned with onion, garlic, and chile powder; and sold by the cupful as *chapulines*, a word that means both "locusts" and, in colloquial Spanish, "kids."

The following recipe for calls for eastern lubber grasshoppers—real whoppers with rose-red wings and black, heavily armored bodies handsomely pinstriped in yellow. You can substitute other lubbers (including the equally large *Brachystola magna*, whose range extends from Minnesota, Montana, and North Dakota into Arizona, Texas, and Mexico). If lubbers are unavailable, any large grasshopper or locust species will suffice.

Although they may look neat, live eastern lubbers can be a real pain in the neck, eating up farmers' profits throughout the southeastern United States. They also pose challenges to insect collectors, frequently hissing and folding and unfolding their wings in a threatening display when approached. Worse yet, live specimens can exude a foul-smelling frothy brown liquid when handled—a reminder that it's not polite to play with your food. Despite their bad habits, lubbers are popular subjects for dissection in high school and college biology classes—and at my dinner table. Prepared like Crispy Crickets (page 29), lubbers make a magnificent finger food. There's no reason to remove the limbs from these handsome devils before cooking them. Show your guests how to snap off and discard the lubber's leathery wing covers and two pairs of forelegs, then invite them to grab hold of a hind leg and give it a yank. There's plenty of meat in each muscular femur, the grasshopper's drumstick, so to speak. Having thus exposed the lubber's long, dark abdomen, it's now time to dig in. *Mucho gusto,* my entomophagous amigos.

---

3 tablespoons vegetable oil

1 clove garlic, finely chopped

1 medium yellow onion, diced

1 pound zucchini, cut into $^1/_2$-inch slices

1 pound tomatoes, peeled and coarsely chopped

2 whole serrano chiles

12 frozen lubber grasshoppers, thawed

Salt and freshly ground pepper to taste

1. Heat the oil in a large skillet over medium heat. Add the garlic and onion and sauté for 1 minute.

2. Add the zucchini, tomatoes, and chiles. Cook, stirring with a wooden spoon, until the zucchini is tender, about 8 to 10 minutes.

3. Gently add the grasshoppers and cover the skillet. Reduce the heat to low and cook for 5 minutes, stirring the mixture from time to time so it doesn't stick to the bottom of the skillet.

4. Season to taste with salt and pepper and serve hot.

ENTO-EPHEMERA

An after-dinner cocktail made from cream, crème de menthe, and white crème de cacao, a Grasshopper can be a real kick.

Travels with My Ant: Yummy or Yucky?

Most of us eat all manner of strange stuff, but if our parents or grandparents served it to us—whether it was pickled pigs feet or oxtail soup—we think everybody should try it. Because we grew up with them, those oddities become our comfort foods. If you were raised in Japan, your comfort foods might include flying fish eggs, seaweed soup, and slivers of raw octopus.

When I present programs to kids, I often bring a rubber chicken with me to wave at the crowds. "What's so glamorous about eating one of these?" I ask the children. Then, in a hushed, conspiratorial tone, I say, "In fact, there are people in this very room who eat what comes out of the *bottom* of one of these birds."

This triggers the twittering, which ends when I say, "Now wait a minute. How many of you had eggs for breakfast?" It's a good joke and it gets them every time. "But if I told you we'd be eating turtle eggs for breakfast tomorrow, you'd freak," I continue, "even though in some parts of the world people have harvested turtle eggs with such zeal that the turtles are in danger of disappearing."

Years ago, before I met my wife, I took a date to a sushi bar in West Seattle. We ordered our favorites—California rolls and *unagi*, or smoked eel, on daikon radish. Desirous of one final delicacy, we asked if the chef would choose something special for us. The nori-wrapped rolls that arrived at our table were delicious, but neither of us recognized their contents.

Our waiter filled us in. "The secret ingredient is *shirako*, or cod milt," he told us.

"What's that?" my date asked.

"It's the stuff Daddy Cod gives Mommy Cod to make Baby Cod," I tactfully replied.

ST. JOHN'S BREAD

Yield: 1 large loaf (serves 6 to 8)

One couldn't ask for a better proponent of bug eating than John the Baptist, the charismatic, if at times enigmatic, forerunner and herald of Jesus Christ.

The Gospel According to Saint Matthew describes how John distanced himself and his disciples from the comforts afforded by cities and towns. He founded his ministry in the harsh "wilderness of Judea" and wore hand-me-downs from an ascetic's closet—a "garment of haircloth, with a girdle of leather about his loins." But while these facts are interesting in themselves, it is John's diet during his days in the desert that seems to have captured the imagination of today's biblical scholars.

According to Matthew, John survived solely on locusts and wild honey. Although this makes perfect sense to bug eaters, many scholars have found his no-frills regimen (dare I say it?) hard to swallow. In their opinion, what sustained John was the carob tree, *Ceratonia siliqua*, a member of the pea family, Leguminosae, which includes many trees commonly called locusts. It is from the fingerlike pods of this particular locust tree that carob, a sweet pulp with a chocolaty taste, has been extracted for well over two thousand years. That carob is also known in some parts of the world as St. John's bread has done little to weaken these scholars' case.

Although carob is undeniably delicious, its food value is not much different than honey. A visionary like John would certainly know better than to base his diet on sweets. Besides, carob trees only grow in moist coastal plains; they are unable to survive the hostile conditions of the desert where John chose to set up camp.

We may never know the real identity of the food that John the Baptist ate. Even the Hebrew words for the two items—*hagavim* for locusts, *haruvim* for locust trees—are sufficiently similar to mix them up in our minds. In the spirit of compromise, then, I offer the following recipe, which calls for both all-natural ingredients.

---

3 tablespoons butter, warmed to room temperature

$1/2$ cup honey

1 teaspoon vanilla extract

6 tablespoons carob powder

$1^1/2$ cups whole-wheat pastry flour

1 teaspoon salt

$1/2$ teaspoon baking soda

$1/2$ teaspoon cream of tartar

1 cup milk

1 cup oven-baked locusts (see instructions for Crispy Crickets on page 29), coarsely chopped

1. Preheat the oven to 350°F. Butter and flour an 8-inch round cake pan.

2. In a large bowl, beat the butter and honey together until fluffy. Stir in the vanilla.

3. In a separate bowl, stir together the carob powder, flour, salt, baking soda, and cream of tartar. Add half the dry ingredients to the butter and honey mixture, then the milk, then the remaining half of the dry ingredients, beating well after each addition.

4. Add the chopped locusts to the bowl and stir to evenly distribute the bug pieces.

5. Pour into the prepared cake pan. Bake until a cake tester inserted into the middle of the cake comes out clean, about 20 minutes.

NOTE: This dish is good any time, but it is best served on June 24, the feast day of Saint John the Baptist.

ENTO-EPHEMERA

After assiduously poring over the Bible looking for references to land arthropods, entomologist W. G. Bruce published his findings in the *Bulletin of the Entomological Society of America* in 1958. His list of 120 citations did not include any references to honey or to manna—a food that many believe came from aphids or scale insects—but it did include several mentions of edible arthropods. My personal favorite: "Or if he shall ask an egg, will he offer him a scorpion?" (Luke 11:12). Here is a list of the most frequently named bugs from the Bible:

Locust: 24	Moth: 11
Grasshopper: 10	Scorpion: 10
Caterpillar: 9	Bee: 4

SHEESH! KABOBS

Yield: 6 servings

Katydids crunch. I learned this while visiting the Sepilok Orangutan Rehabilitation Centre in Malaysian Borneo, where I spied a young orangutan firmly grasping the large body of an adult forest katydid with the toes of his left foot. Demonstrating a degree of flexibility that would put my yoga instructor to shame, the rust-colored primate slowly raised his foot until it was level with his mouth. Then came the sound, a celerylike crunch, as the orang's molars came down on the katydid's thorax and head.

Our closest relatives, the great apes, are all avid insect eaters. The feeding habits of chimpanzees have been especially well documented because of these animals' use of tools—twigs stripped of their leaves—for extracting edible termites from mounds. I've read that using such tools may take up as much as 30 percent of a chimp's food-seeking time.

The bug-eating biases of another great ape, the mountain gorilla, have also been well documented. "I was amazed to see the two captives ignore such treats as blackberries to search for worms and grubs," primate specialist Dian Fossey wrote of two orphaned infants, Coco and Pucker, in her book *Gorillas in the Mist*. She continues, "They often appeared to know exactly where to peel the slabs from live and dead tree trunks to find abundant deposits of larvae. Even while licking one slab clean, purring with pleasure over their feast, they were ripping off another slab for more burrowed protein sources." Some primates, such as the Malayan spectral lemur, produce chitinase, an enzyme that allows them to digest the exoskeletons of arthropods. Because humans have limited abilities to digest chitin (and lack the die-hard dentition of chimpanzees or gorillas), we rely on culinary tricks to overcome the chitinous crunch.

Marinating is the best way I know to tenderize the tough skins of food arthropods. To be effective at softening exoskeletons, the marinade must be highly acidic, strengthened with vinegar or lemon juice. Even with marinade, the outer armor of many arthropods isn't easily penetrated. For this reason I recommend using metal or sturdy presoaked wood skewers with arrow-sharp tips.

In this recipe an assortment of orthopterans is marinated, skewered, and suspended over a bed of hot coals. Our earliest human ancestors probably cooked bugs this way, although they may not have had marinade, Dijon mustard, or, for that matter, any real need to presoften chitin. It's easy to connect with the spirits of long-gone *Homo erectus* and *Australopithecus*, both arthropod eaters extraordinaire, while you poke at the embers, readying your Weber or hibachi for the next round of edible bugs.

continued

MARINADE

$1/_2$ cup fresh lemon juice

1 tablespoon olive oil

1 teaspoon honey

$1/_2$ teaspoon freshly grated ginger

1 tablespoon Dijon mustard

2 tablespoons minced fresh herbs, such as parsley, mint, thyme, and tarragon

$1/_4$ teaspoon salt

Pinch of freshly ground pepper

12 frozen katydids, grasshoppers, or other large-bodied Orthoptera, thawed

1 red bell pepper, cut into $1^1/_2$-inch chunks

1 small yellow onion, cut into 8 wedges

COOKING TIP

Pierce the thorax and abdomen of a large-bodied edible insect with the tines of a small fork—a procedure that is easiest to perform while the insect's body is still frozen. This will allow the marinade to enter the insect, imparting its flavor while working away at the chitin from the inside. The holes don't have to be large or deep. In fact, smaller punctures are less likely to damage organ meats or permit the insect's precious bodily fluids to drain out.

1. Mix all ingredients for the marinade in a nonreactive baking dish. Add the katydids, cover, and marinate in the refrigerator overnight.

2. When ready to cook, remove the katydids from the marinade and pat dry. Assemble the kabobs by alternately skewering the insects, bell pepper, and onion wedges to create a visually interesting lineup.

3. Brush the grill lightly with olive oil. Cook the kabobs 2 or 3 inches above the fire, turning them every two or three minutes and basting them with additional olive oil as required. The exact cooking time will vary, depending on your grill and the type of insects used. However, the kabobs should cook for no longer than 8 or 9 minutes.

REALLY HOPPIN' JOHN

Yield: 4 to 6 servings

Hoppin' John is a traditional Southern delight that in recent years has caught the attention of diners across America. Typically served on New Year's Day, this savory stew is thought to bring good luck for the coming year.

My version of this classic entrée is particularly appropriate to usher in a leap year (get it?). The handsome green conehead grasshoppers are both decorative and scrumptious, with a woodsy taste not unlike hazelnuts. They are seasonally abundant throughout the South, making them an appropriate regional accent for the rice, black-eyed peas, and cayenne pepper used in this dish.

As a substitute for coneheads, try any of the smaller, more common short-horned grasshoppers (family Acrididae), familiar inhabitants of meadows and roadsides throughout the United States and Canada, or use Crispy Crickets (page 29), which are nearly as tasty and much easier to obtain.

12 frozen conehead grasshoppers or 24 Crispy Crickets (page 29)

2 cups cooked black-eyed peas

2 cups cooked long-grain rice

2 tablespoons butter or vegetable oil

1 medium yellow onion, diced

2 garlic cloves, minced

Pinch of ground allspice

Pinch of cayenne pepper

Salt and freshly ground pepper to taste

1 large tomato, chopped

1 tablespoon finely chopped fresh parsley

1. Set aside two grasshoppers to garnish the completed dish. While the remaining grasshoppers are still frozen, remove their wings, wing covers, and forelegs.

2. In a small saucepan, heat the black-eyed peas until warm. In a separate small saucepan, add 3 tablespoons water to the cooked rice, cover, and rewarm briefly over low heat.

3. In a 12-inch cast-iron skillet, warm the butter or oil. Add the onion and garlic and sauté until golden, about 10 minutes. Add the grasshoppers. Season with allspice and cayenne. Stir in the black-eyed peas and rice.

4. Add salt and pepper to taste. Sprinkle with the chopped tomato and parsley. Cover and heat through for 8 to 10 minutes. Do not overcook; each ingredient should retain its individual identity, flavor, and texture. Garnish with the two whole grasshoppers and serve. Your guests will be jumping with joy.

CHAPULINES CON CHOCOLATE FONDUE

Yield: 8 servings

The inspiration for this recipe hit me while I was visiting Switzerland, where, in the spring of 2012, I was invited to cook at the Inter-Community School in Zurich. One day, while indulging my fondness for all forms of Swiss chocolate, I had a thought: with the current trendiness of salted caramels and other sweets, why not a salted chocolate that combines *chapulines*—the small baked and seasoned grasshoppers from Mexico—with a chocolate fondue from the Alps?

If you live in a city with a large Hispanic population, then you may have access to *chapulines* from Oaxaca, Mexico. I usually shop for them in Los Angeles, where they are often sold in plastic bags at Oaxacan-owned grocery stores, often for about $7 for 30 grams. Sometimes you'll get lucky and find *chapulines* at Oaxacan restaurants as well. Because these may not be listed on the menu, you might have to request them from your waiter. That's what I do whenever I dine at La Carta de Oaxaca in Seattle's Ballard neighborhood.

Before they are sold, the small grasshoppers are boiled, toasted on a *comal* (a clay cooking surface), and sprinkled with garlic, lime, and salt. The salt is said to contain the extract of *gusano*, or the caterpillars of a moth, *Hypopta agavis*, that lays its eggs on the same agave plant that mescal is made from. *Gusanos*, by the way, are often included in bottles of this beverage to enhance its taste and establish its authenticity. I encourage you to drink some mescal before, during, and after you try my recipe. Trust me on this one: mescal (or its close relative, tequila) and dark chocolate are a great combination—and *chapulines* are an addition that only strengthens that bond.

$^3/_4$ cup half-and-half

$^3/_4$ cup heavy cream

$1^1/_2$ pounds semiweet chocolate morsels

1 tablespoon ground cinnamon

1 teaspoon ancho chile powder

$^1/_3$ cup Kahlúa

32 chapuline grasshoppers

1. In a conventional fondue pot, double boiler, or electric fondue maker, combine the half-and-half and heavy cream. Warm on medium-heat until small bubbles begin to form around the edges.

2. Reduce the heat slightly and gradually add the chocolate, whisking after each addition to melt the chocolate and thoroughly combine.

3. When chocolate is completely blended, add the cinnamon, chile powder, and Kahlúa.

4. Pierce individual *chapulines* with 6-inch bamboo skewers, then dip each small grasshopper into the chocolate mixture.

5. Allow the chocolate-covered *chapulines* to cool slightly before eating.

PART TWO

TOGETHERNESS

A Selection of Social Insects
for Special Occasions

> "For among Bees and Ants are social systems found so complex and well-order'd as to invite offhand a pleasant fable enough: that once upon a time, or ever a man were born to rob their honeypots, bees were fully endow'd with Reason and only lost it by ordering so their life as to dispense with it; whereby it pined away and perish'd of disuse."
> —Robert Bridges (1844–1930)

Many land arthropods like to hang out together. However, only members of the orders Hymenoptera (ants, bees, and wasps) and Neuroptera (termites) do so for a greater good. Known to scientists as eusocial (or truly social) insects, these animals cooperate to raise their young collectively. They parcel out certain tasks, such as reproduction and collecting food, throughout the entire group. Better still, they are the only arthropods to exhibit genuinely altruistic behavior. In other words, they will lay down their lives if necessary so that others of their kind will survive. Land arthropods that exhibit only a few of these exemplary traits are called subsocial animals. I wonder how we would rate on this scale.

The advantages of eusociality are many. By working together on projects—building a hive, for instance—eusocial insects can accomplish far greater things than they could on their own. Such insects are also better at defending themselves against the attacks of much bigger animals. (Ever try to get rid of a hornet's nest?) Plus, there's a better chance of raising another generation when there are plenty of assistants to keep their compound eyes on the kids. Eusocial insects can also horde far great reserves of food than their subsocial kin, a real evolutionary advantage, as illustrated by Aesop's fable about the ant and the grasshopper.

We benefit from the eusocial behaviors of bees whenever we spread honey on our English muffins. We suffer the consequences of eusociality if we buy termite-infested real estate or stand in the way of a platoon of carnivorous army ants. However, only a wildlife ecologist would know how very important to our world these small creatures are—as plant pollinators, recyclers of dead plant material, and industrious tillers of the soil.

FOOD FOR THOUGHT

- Beeswax, bee pollen, propolis (the sticky exudation for coating the inside of a bee hive), and, of course, honey are all edible products manufactured by bees.
- "Go to the ant, thou sluggard, consider her ways and be wise" is just one of nine references to social insects in the Bible.
- Colonial wasps are avid bug eaters. In one hour the adults may collect more than two hundred insects to feed the hungry larvae in their colony.
- North American homesteaders placed cornbread crumbs around cucumber plants, attracting ants that they hoped would kill cucumber pests.
- The female velvet ant is wingless and covered with red or yellow fuzz. But don't let looks fool you: she's really a wasp.

CHAPTER 3

TANTALIZING TERMITES (THE OTHER WHITE MEAT)

> **"** The termites are prepared for the table by various methods, some persons pounding them so as to form them into a kind of soft paste, while others roast them like coffee beans or chestnuts. **"** —Reverend J. G. Wood, *Illustrated Natural History* (1863)

The towering termite nests of the African plain are not unlike our own golden arches—highly visible symbols of speedy service and quick hunger relief. A single nest of African termites may house as many as three million individuals from several different castes, including workers, soldiers, and so-called "winged reproductives."

Unlike their wingless (and often sightless) nest mates, the members of this last caste can flutter about. At various times of the year they leave the nest in great clouds, dispersing themselves, then shedding their wings and settling down. They pair off, mate, and start new colonies over which they will rule as king and queen.

During the earliest stages of colony formation, the reproductives take care of business by themselves. They feed the first batch of babies until they are big enough to serve. Then both king and queen enjoy the good life for the remainder of their days, which for the queens of some species can number in the thousands. Every termite in the colony is a direct descendant of this pair—so I shouldn't have to tell you what the king and queen do with all that free time.

The other termite castes aren't able to reproduce, so they apply their energies to making the world a better place—for termites, that is. Workers are responsible for building the maze of tunnels and chambers in which everybody lives. They also feed and groom the other members of the colony.

A soldier's sole chore is to defend the colony, and it takes its job quite seriously. "These born gladiators seem to exult in war," writes our buddy Reverend J. G. Wood in his *Illustrated Natural History*, who also notes, "No matter what may be the size of the assailant, they hurry to the attack with reckless fury, biting fiercely with their sharp jaws."

The indigenous peoples of the world have subsisted on termites, especially the comparatively large-bodied reproductives, for many centuries. Native South Americans, Australians, and Africans all employ similar strategies for snaring their share of the swarms. At

HARVESTING HINT

Most Western diners have little to fear from a fat-rich diet of termites, whose flavor has been compared to both hazelnuts and sweetened cream. Finding a good source of these victuals can pose problems, however, as termite nests in most northern forests are neither as conspicuous nor as densely populated as those of equatorial lands. Still, if they time their search correctly, prospective termite eaters can find whitish, smokelike streams of winged reproductives emanating from tree stumps and large rotting logs.

the right time of year (usually the start of the rainy season), they wrap the termite nests in a shroud of leaves, fabric, or grasses, and then they pick off the emerging winged termites, which now must struggle to reach the not-so-friendly skies.

The author of *Insects as Human Food*, Israeli entomophage F. S. Bodenheimer, compares the anticipation of the rainy season in central Africa to "the hailing of the advent of the oyster season by British gourmets." He describes at length the harvest of winged termites by the Baganda people, who devour these large and luxuriously rich insects alive. When the termites leave the nests ("a contingency which has long been foreseen," as the Israeli entomophage puts it), they collide with a sheet of bark cloth, which is carefully spread over the summit of the termite hill.

"The impact," writes Bodenheimer, "breaks off their wings at the sutures and they fall to the ground within the curtain in white, struggling masses; their wings are swept aside by human hands, when they are sifted out from the cloth. Men and women scoop them up in handfuls, eating a few occasionally, savoring the flavor; naked children, shrieking with delight, vie with all the birds of the neighborhood, wild or tame, in chasing and collecting stragglers, munching as they run, stuffing themselves to repletion, heedless of the acute diarrhoea which will presently disorganize their interiors."

The intestinal distress that Bodenheimer describes could be attributed to the termites' iron-rich bodies, or perhaps to the sudden infusion of fat (identified as 36.2 percent and 44.4 percent in two separate laboratory analyses) in the African children's ordinarily lean diets.

For *Reticulitermes flavipes*, the most common species in eastern North America, mass takeoffs typically occur in the spring. In many western species (including a pair of chestnut-headed coastal residents, *Zootermopsis angusticollis* and *nevadensis*), such flights are scheduled for late summer months.

Armed with a long-handled butterfly net, one can swiftly collect enough winged termites to make any number of simple but elegant bug dishes. If you're really lucky and happen to live near a greenbelt or forest preserve, the flying termites may occasionally come to you, flitting in through the open windows of your kitchen in search of mates and the best places for making their nests. In this case, it's a good idea to fry up these intruders on the spot, preventing their offspring from making a meal out of the untreated wood in your home.

ENTO-EPHEMERA

Writing of the Uele district in what is now the Democratic Republic of Congo, J. C. Bequaert described how both the Azande and Mangbetu people considered the region's tall termite mounds private property. During the harvest of edible insect inhabitants, fights often broke out among rival claimants. Such skirmishes over termites occasionally had fatal outcomes, according to the well-traveled Bequaert.

If you can't find winged termites, you might have to settle for the smaller workers and soldiers. You can always bust open a rotten log and collect them yourself (but be careful to keep any exposed skin from the soldiers' jaws), or you can order termites through the mail, from the suppliers in the Resources section of this book (page 120). Whether cooking with wild or store-bought livestock, freeze your specimens immediately, nipping any chances of home-wrecking infestations in the bud.

CURRIED TERMITE STEW

Yield: 6 servings

Throughout Africa winged termites are roasted, fried, or eaten raw. Part of the cooking procedure involves stripping the termites of their wings by sprinkling them with water or tossing them into a water-filled pot. Thus readied, the insects are usually cooked by themselves and occasionally salted for later consumption. There's your authentic recipe.

To make more of a production out of the termite-eating experience, however, I suggest the following approach, freely adapted from *The Enchanted Broccoli Forest*, by Mollie Katzen. Her recipe for Curried Peanut Soup is appropriately African for the addition of dewinged reproductive termites. However, I've reduced both the number and the quantities of the spices Katzen recommends, since who wants to obliterate the taste of termites in this hearty stew?

1 tablespoon butter

2 large cloves garlic, crushed

1 cup chopped yellow onion

2 tablespoons freshly grated ginger

1 cup raw peanuts, chopped

20 winged reproductive termites, wings removed

1 teaspoon salt

$^1/_4$ teaspoon *each* cinnamon, coriander, cumin, dry mustard, and turmeric

$1^1/_2$ cups water

$^1/_2$ cup creamy peanut butter

1 tablespoon honey

Fresh lemon juice for serving

1. In a medium stockpot over medium heat, melt the butter, then sauté the garlic, onion, ginger, peanuts, and termites. Add the salt and seasonings, reduce the heat and cook for 8 to 10 minutes, stirring occasionally.

2. Add the water, peanut butter, and honey to the stockpot. Stir to combine, reduce the heat to low, cover, and simmer for 30 to 40 minutes.

3. Ladle the stew into small bowls. Add a dash of lemon juice to each portion immediately before serving.

HARVESTING HINT

Even tiny termites have big jaws. If you're ordering termites by mail, request workers, which are a bit smaller than soldiers but lack the ability to bite back. They're about half the price, too—around thirty or forty cents apiece. If tempted to eat a soldier termite alive (and I don't recommend it, because of their sharp mandibles), make your first bite count, crushing the insect's head before it can latch onto the delicate tissue of the lips, tongue, or lining of the mouth.

TERMITE TREATS

Yield: 16 bars

Watch how quickly these between-meal snacks disappear from your kitchen. You may never make this dish without the termites again.

The termites are the only decent source of nutrition in these familiar treats. If you're watching your weight, don't eat too many of them: an ounce of live termites contains around 100 calories. That's roughly the same number of calories in four marshmallows.

4 teaspoons margarine

20 large marshmallows (about 5 ounces)

$2^1/_2$ cups crispy rice cereal

Vegetable oil

$^1/_2$ cup oven-baked termites, either soldiers, workers, or reproductives (see instructions for Crispy Crickets on page 29)

1. In a saucepan over low heat, melt the margarine. Add the marshmallows and stir until melted. Remove from the heat.

2. Add the crispy rice cereal. Stir until the cereal is evenly coated with the marshmallow mixture.

3. Lightly coat an 8 by 8-inch baking pan with vegetable oil. With a lightly buttered spatula or wax paper, press the mixture into the baking pan. Top with the termites, pressing them into the surface of the melted marshmallow and crispy rice mix.

4. Allow to cool, then cut into 2-inch squares. Stand back.

ENTO-EPHEMERA

Early Spanish settlers in Brazil hollowed out termite nests and turned them into ovens. In the East Indies, according to entomologist Lucy Clausen, queen termites are eaten by old men to "affect rejuvenation and a strengthening of the back."

CHAPTER 4

BEGINNING WITH BEES

Everybody loves honey, but how many of us like honeybees? Plenty of people, according to F. S. Bodenheimer, who singles out the Mbuti Pygmies of Africa's Ituri Forest, the Lao of northern Thailand, Timor islanders of Indonesia, and Khoisan of South Africa in his seminal study *Insects as Human Food*. If we include the eaters of honeybee larvae and pupae—the two types of bees-to-be, as it were—we can add diners in Australia, Malaysia, India, China, and Japan to Bodenheimer's list.

Adult honeybees are roughly 15 percent protein. Their pupae are even more protein-rich (about 18 percent), making them comparable to lamb and a little better than pork in this department. Adult bees are also laden with amino acids, especially lysine and methionine. Because corn is deficient in these basic building blocks of life, it's been suggested that adult bees would make a superb additive to the feed of farm-raised, corn-fed hogs.

Larval and pupal honeybees are soft-bodied and exceptionally palatable. Their inherent sweetness is due, no doubt, to the nurturing diet of royal jelly (a highly nutritious tonic from the hypopharyngeal, or throat, glands of adult bees) on which these insects are reared.

The real benefits of bee eating, though, are from the vitamins stored by these tiny beasts. Honey contains an assortment of B vitamins (no pun intended) plus appreciable quantities of vitamins C and E. Although the bodies of honeybee larvae and pupae contain meager amounts of these substances, they are chock-full of vitamins A and D. One nutritional study has confirmed that a larval honeybee may contain fifteen times the recommended daily allowance of these two vitamins. Taken over extended periods, $2^1/_2$ tablespoons of honeybee larvae per day can induce symptoms of vitamin D toxicity, leading to serious side effects such as calcification of blood vessel walls and the hardening of soft tissues of the heart.

Steering Clear of Stings

"You gotta be careful of dead bees," purrs Lauren Bacall in the classic film *To Have and Have Not*. "They can sting ya just as bad as live ones, especially if they was kinda mad when they got killed."

Yes, dear readers, it is possible to get stung by dead Hymenoptera. As long as the sharp barb remains attached to the business end of a bee or a wasp, there will be a chance of being stung, even if the insect has shuffled off its mortal coil.

To be on the safe side, remove the stingers of large bees or wasps before cooking with them. This is best accomplished with the aid of small tweezers. With the fingers of one hand, grasp the insect firmly by its abdomen. Gently squeeze, causing the stinger to protrude from the animal's rear end. Now use the tweezers to clamp down on the stinger and, with a rapid jerk of the wrist, pluck the stinger and its attached venom gland free. You have now defused your food.

Stings from dead bees can be avoided altogether if you acquire only drones, the stingerless "princes" of a hive. These insects are easily recognized by their long wings, which extend to the tip of the abdomen. They're much larger and clumsier than their cohorts, and their buzzing is louder and at a slightly different pitch. During the breeding and swarming season, hundreds and sometimes thousands of these barbless buddies can be taken from a single hive.

Should you or your guests get stung by a bee before, during, or after a meal, remain calm. Usually, the initial pain will dissipate within minutes. While there may be some swelling or redness around the wound, it's seldom necessary to do anything but apply a cold compress.

On rare occasions, though, victims of bee stings may have allergic reactions, especially if they've suffered multiple stings or single stings on several consecutive days. Occasionally sting victims may have delayed reactions a week or two after the initial incident. Symptoms can include nausea, dizziness, headache, difficulty in breathing, or a drop in blood pressure. Should you observe any of these symptoms, seek immediate medical help. If you have reason to believe you might be allergic to bee stings, please skip the recipes in this part of the book.

Bounteous Bees

Adult honeybees and their larvae and pupae are available throughout the spring and summer months in northern climes. In the southern states, they may be obtained year-round.

The best way to secure your share of honeybees is by befriending your local apiculturists, that is, beekeepers. Start off by purchasing some of their honey—there are certainly worse ways to spend your time and money. Having established your worth (in economic terms anyway), it's okay to ask if you can see the hives where the liquid ambrosia was made.

While on your site tour, drop a few hints ("Say, those are mighty tasty looking bees"). Tell your new friend about the dietary practices of the Mbuti Pygmies and Timor islanders. Then ask if you can purchase some drones or a few squares of the comb with the pupae and larvae still in them. That's how I first met beekeeper Les Tavenner, who for many years proved instrumental in supplying me with honeybees from all stages of life.

I need to note that the health of our bees has been threatened on a number of fronts in recent years. Introduced parasites and predators of honeybees have taken their toll on once-healthy hives, and conversion of prairies and pastures into sites for suburban homes has done away with many of the native bees' traditional stomping grounds. Because of this, all bees are in need of our protection to a degree. Readers will be surprised to learn that the ubiquitous honeybee is not native to North America, and that all of the native bee species in our part of the world live solitary, not colonial, lives. For this reason, I am directing any bug chefs in training to focus on bees born to apiculturists, from well-tended hives.

ENTO-EPHEMERA

Japan's traditional wasp catchers tie a long silk thread to the waist of an adult wasp, then follow the insect back to its nest. Once the nest is located, the wasp catchers use smoke to drive the adults away and then harvest the edible larvae.

GLORY BEE

Yield: 4 servings

The traditional Buddhist prohibition against eating four-legged beasts may have encouraged the incorporation of insects into Japanese cuisine in the years predating contact with the West. Even today, even in the most heavily Westernized sectors of Tokyo, you can find an assortment of canned arthropod treats. On assignment for Japan's *Sinra* magazine, a trio of visiting journalists once brought me an assortment pack of tinned larval bees, stream insects, and grasshoppers in teriyaki sauce—all delicacies in their homeland.

The following recipe is my attempt to re-create the classic bug cuisine of Japan. Its harmonious balance of flavors evokes the quest for the middle ground—an ancient tenet of Japanese Buddhism.

2 tablespoons butter

1 tablespoon minced garlic

$^1/_2$ cup roasted cashews

2 cups frozen adult honeybee drones, thawed

$^1/_4$ cup dry white wine

1 tablespoon light soy sauce

1 teaspoon brown sugar

Freshly ground pepper to taste

Cooked long-grain brown rice for serving

1. In a large skillet over medium-high heat, melt the butter. Add the garlic, cashews, and honeybee drones. Cook, stirring, for 2 or 3 minutes, until the cashews soften and the garlic turns golden brown.

2. Add the wine and decrease the heat to medium, simmering until wine is reduced and flavors have mingled, about 4 or 5 minutes.

3. Add the soy sauce and brown sugar and season with pepper. Remove from the heat and serve on a bed of rice.

COOKING TIP

It seems like every bug eater has a different trick for extracting bee larvae and pupae from their sealed hexagonal compartments in the comb. Some recommend taking a knife and carefully scraping away the wax lids, then flushing out the contents with a trickle of cold water directed across the top of the comb. Others tell me to drop the entire comb into hot water and skim the larvae from the melted wax soup

The easiest method I've found involves freezing the comb and its contents, then breaking the compartments apart, one row at a time, to release the frozen larvae. The little ivory-colored bodies can be collected, cleaned of any superfluous wax, and either returned to the freezer or plunged into boiling water for immediate use.

THREE BEE SALAD

Yield: 4 servings

This nontraditional salad combines the best of the bee world: the vitamin-rich larvae and pupae, plus the high-protein adult bees. As a bonus, I've added a few sprinkles of bee pollen, also known as beebread, the sweet-tasting granules that have been harvested from flowers by these busy, eusocial beings.

The dish owes its appeal to the combination of tastes and textures contributed by the three principal ingredients. As such, extra care must be taken to avoid bruising the larvae and pupae. A soft bamboo tea strainer should be used for removing these ingredients from their boiling water bath. A chopstick or small wooden spoon works well for combining the tender bee babies with the hard-bodied adults.

Bee pollen will gradually disintegrate if it floats for very long in the marinade. Add this ingredient only when you are ready to bring the dish to the table. Did you know that in order to gather one load of beebread (two granules), a bee must visit something like three hundred clover flowers? Or that ten such loads are needed to raise a bee from egg to adulthood? No wonder these insects are so busy, and that bee pollen sells for upward of $2 an ounce.

$1/_2$ cup (about 40) frozen adult bees

$1/_2$ cup (about 60) frozen bee pupae

$1/_2$ cup (about 60) frozen bee larvae

2 tablespoons red wine vinegar

6 tablespoons olive oil

1 teaspoon Dijon mustard

Salt and freshly ground pepper to taste

1 ounce bee pollen granules

Lettuce for serving

Nasturtium petals or other edible flowers for serving

1. Bring two quarts of lightly salted water to a boil. Add the adult honeybees and return to boil for 1 minute. Using a slotted spoon, remove the bees from the water. Pat dry with paper towels and allow to cool.

2. To the same water, add the honeybee pupae. Repeat the procedure for cooking the adult bees (but watch how you pat these little guys with the paper towels!), also allowing the pupae to cool.

3. Repeat the same process with the honeybee larvae.

4. In a large bowl, combine the vinegar, oil, mustard, and salt and pepper to taste. Add the cooked adult bees, followed by the pupae, then the larvae.

5. Immediately before serving, add the bee pollen granules, stirring the mixture to ensure that the granules are evenly distributed.

6. Serve on a bed of lettuce, decorated with the nasturtium petals, a bee-utiful touch for this bee-atific dish.

BEE'S KNEES

Yield: 8 servings of 2 "knees" each

I've always felt that Ronald Taylor and Barbara Carter missed the boat by not including any actual insects in their recipe for Honey Bee Granola Bars, one of several interesting desserts (and, in this case, a clever reworking of traditional noninsect energy bars) in *Entertaining with Insects*. So here I am, embellishing on their early effort. The title of this dish is taken from the hipster's slang of my mother's generation. Mom liked anything with coconut in it, so this one's for her.

1$^1/_2$ cups sifted all-purpose flour
1$^1/_3$ cups firmly packed brown sugar
1 teaspoon baking powder
1 teaspoon salt
2 tablespoons milk
2 large eggs, beaten
1 teaspoon vanilla extract
$^1/_2$ cup chopped walnuts
$^1/_2$ cup sunflower seeds
$^1/_2$ cup shredded coconut
$^1/_2$ cup sesame seeds
$^3/_4$ cup (about 90) frozen bee pupae, thawed
$^1/_2$ cup (4 ounces) bee pollen granules

1. Preheat the oven to 325°F and grease a 13 by 9-inch baking dish well.

2. In a large mixing bowl, sift together the flour, brown sugar, baking powder, and salt. Slowly mix in the milk, eggs, and vanilla followed by the walnuts, sunflower seeds, coconut, and sesame seeds. Gently fold in the bee pupae and pollen granules.

3. Turn the batter into the prepared pan. Bake until a cake tester comes out clean, about 30 minutes.

4. Remove from the oven and let cool. With a sharp knife, cut into 9 rectangles, each 4 by 3 inches, then divide each rectangle into two L-shaped pieces—the bee's "knees."

5. Artfully arrange the pieces on a platter and set out for all to enjoy. Your kids will think these Bee's Knees are the cat's pajamas, or the snake's hips, as my mom would say.

CHAPTER 5

ANTS ON (AND IN) THE HOUSE

The ant has made himself illustrious
Through constant industry industrious
So what?
Would you be calm and placid,
If you were full of formic acid?
  —Ogden Nash

What's a picnic without ants? There are some eight thousand described species of these fellas and possibly another thirty thousand waiting to be identified. In many places, including tropical rain forests and arid lands, ants outnumber all other terrestrial animals.

The physical adaptations and behaviors of ants are highly varied and complex. Ant society, like that of termites, is driven by the caste system; as many as twelve million helpers may be actively engaged in their predetermined roles for the overall good of the colony.

Like their hymenopteran kin (bees, hornets, and wasps), ants are favored fare wherever they abound—which, as I've already established, is pretty much everywhere. The winged nobility, both males and females, are captured and prepared in much the same manner as termites. Workers and soldiers of many ant species are also conveniently bite-sized.

Several clever strategies are employed to harvest ants before they voluntarily leave the nest. My favorite technique belongs to the Yupka tribe of eastern Colombia. These creative gourmands dig a moat around the entrance to the ants' underground nest. As rainwater fills the moat, it eventual flows into the nest's main entrance, causing the alarmed ants to rapidly evacuate their digs. The escapees can't really go anywhere, because they are trapped by the moat, so the Yupka can collect this insect bounty at a leisurely pace, selectively harvesting the large females, which are bloated with eggs.

"Enough ants are usually collected at one time to fill several small baskets," reported Kenneth Ruddle in a 1973 issue of the scientific journal *Biotropica*. "Individual handfuls of ants are wrapped in leaves and placed on a log close to the fire to roast."

Ant-Acid

Ants secrete formic acid, a mildly caustic compound with a urinelike odor that has inspired both the scientific name for their family, the Formicidae, and the archaic terms for the critters "pismire" and "pissant." By following the scent of formic acid laid down by troop leaders, ants can walk single file through the dense jungle or across cluttered kitchen countertops without ever getting lost. The same acid in a more concentrated form gives ant bites their potent sting.

HARVESTING HINT

When cooking, I like to use the local ant fauna, especially *Formica obscuripes*, the mahogany-colored western thatching ant, which are easily collected as the workers flow in and out of their nests. I've used a battery-powered handheld vacuum cleaner to scoop up ants several dozen at a time. A word of caution: Use rubber bands or masking tape to seal off the openings to your sleeves to prevent any defenders of the ant colony from gaining access to your skin. After I empty the contents, debris and all, into a large plastic storage container or glass jar, I place the container or jar in the freezer for several hours. When everything is frozen solid, I sort the ants from the pine needles, bits of soil, and other unwanted items.

Formic acid is also what gives ants their vinegarlike flavor—a taste that goes nicely with potato chips and craft beers. Different ant species have varying flavors. I'm told that in North Queensland, Australia, a refreshing beverage is made from the mashed bodies of green weaver ants (*Polyrhachis* sp.) mixed with water. In the south of Mexico, the species of choice is *Atta cephalotes*, whose winged forms are both roasted and boiled. In other parts of Mexico, the little red *Corixa femorata*'s rice-sized larvae are fried in butter or served up in savory stews.

ANT JEMIMA'S BUCKWHEAT–BUG GRIDDLECAKES

Yield: 4 servings

For this recipe use carpenter ants (*Camponotus pennsylvanicus*), the same species that are probably burrowing in the wood-framed walls of Aunt Jemima's original country home. You can substitute the Modoc carpenter ant (*Camponotus modoc*) or the bicolored carpenter ant (*Camponotus vicinus*), if you prefer.

Unlike termites, none of these three species can digest the cellulose in wood. The holes that they drill are nests within which a seemingly endless supply of pancake enhancements may dwell.

1 cup buckwheat flour

2$^1/_2$ teaspoons baking powder

$^1/_2$ teaspoon salt

$^1/_4$ cup whole milk

1 cup water

1 tablespoon blackstrap molasses

$^1/_4$ cup (200 large-bodied or 500 small-bodied) frozen ants, thawed

Vegetable oil for cooking

Maple syrup for serving

Butter for serving

1. In a large bowl, combine the buckwheat flour, baking powder, and salt. Add the milk, water, and molasses and stir until thoroughly blended and there are no lumps. Fold in the ants, distributing them uniformly throughout the batter.

2. Grease a griddle well with vegetable oil and heat over medium-high heat. In batches, ladle the batter onto the griddle to form griddle cakes about 4 inches in diameter. To score extra points, try making three-lobed shapes—head, thorax, and abdomen—as you pour the batter. Cook the griddle cakes, turning once, until browned on both sides.

3. Serve with maple syrup and plenty of butter. You'll be the king (or queen) of the breakfast table.

AMARETTO HONEYPOTS

Yield: 6 servings of 3 ants each

Filled with sweetness, honeypot ants are the crème de la crème of the insect world. Exceptionally large and limber individuals are selected from the worker caste to serve as live storage casks for nectar and honeydew, the sticky secretion harvested from aphids and scale insects. These sugar-rich materials are carried to the nest in the throat sacs (crops) of other workers and fed to the storage-cask ants, whose abdomens become round and distended as they are filled. The technical term for the big-assed ants is "rotunds" or "repletes."

In a colony there may be as many as several thousand of these nectar-filled fatties, the collective's insurance that there will always be food and drink, even in the leanest and driest of seasons. Stuffed to the point of bursting (the honey-sweet nectar can outweigh the ant by a factor of eight), the repletes are completely immobile. They remain for the rest of their lives in specially constructed underground cavities, where they cling to the ceiling with their feet.

If you're hungering for honeypot ants, be prepared to dig deep, for the majority of them live in arid, sun-drenched regions, where the best way to escape the scorching heat is by tunneling far beneath the soil. To acquire his colony of *M. mimicus* for display at the Butterfly Pavilion and Insect Center in Westminster, Colorado, my good friend Michael Weissmann traveled to the outskirts of Tucson, Arizona, where he rented a backhoe for a day. It cost Michael's institution several hundred dollars, but, after twelve hours of digging, the investment paid off with three queens and hundreds of repletes, the majority of which were transferred to a system of simulated burrows in the pavilion's main arthropod wing.

I got my honeypots without any of the muss or fuss. Rather than roll up my sleeves and head for Tucson, I purchased some of Michael's leftovers from Barney Tomberlin of Hatari Invertebrates, the same firm that supplies me with centipedes and scorpions for many of my recipes. The ants arrived on my doorstep in a small container within a well-padded Styrofoam box, carried by a friendly UPS worker. They were a bit bedraggled from their two days on the road, but no worse for wear than if I had dug them up and hand-carried them to my abode in Washington state.

I'm tempted to begin my instructions for Amaretto Honeypots with the phrase, "With a backhoe, dig a fourteen-foot trench in the desert. . . ." On a more practical note, I probably should explain how to eat a freshly killed honeypot ant. Simply hold the head and thorax of the insect between the forefinger and thumb. Now bite down on the abdomen, letting the nectar run into your mouth. Discard the drained insect. Pretty good, isn't it?

continued

18 honeypot ant repletes

$1/2$ cup Amaretto di Saronno or similar liqueur

3 cups shaved ice

1. Dispatch the honeypot ants by freezing them. Remove the ants from the freezer and gently drop them in the amaretto. Let the ants and amaretto warm to room temperature overnight.

2. Immediately before serving, drain the ants and discard the amaretto. Scoop shaved ice into six sherbet dishes. Carefully place three ants, heads up, on each mound of ice.

3. Demonstrate for your guests how to get the full enjoyment from this refreshingly different treat.

Travels with My Ant: Kids—More Adventurous than Their Folks?

If bugs are the food of the future, as some visionary scientists maintain, then our children will become the real beneficiaries of this underutilized resource. That's one reason why I'm pleased by how well elementary and middle school students have received my cooking programs.

Weeks before I'm scheduled to make an appearance at a school, the buzz about eating bugs begins to build, with kids dividing themselves into two camps: those who are excited and those who express their disdain for what they *think* is going to happen when I arrive. More often than not, however, my reception is largely favorable, and I've been known to get a fair number of converts from the opposing camp after an assembly.

When I'm cooking I often invite kids from the audience to help make and sample my dishes. Sometimes the same kids who will gulp down grasshoppers will refuse to eat the mushrooms in a dish.

The reactions from parents are interesting too. "I can't believe my kid volunteered to eat mealworms," a mother will confide. "I can't get him to eat *anything* at home."

Of course your kid doesn't want to eat anything you're giving him, I think. And I'm willing to bet that you're not serving him anything unexpected for lunch or dinner. All too often parents build their meals around what we assume are kid-friendly staples, such as peanut butter and jelly or mac and cheese. For gosh sakes, people, try something different.

During a show I presented at Powell Gardens in Kingsville, Missouri, I attracted one especially ambitious young eater. Probably a preteen, this guy kept returning to my table to grab a sample of crickets and pasta. After his fifth taste, I leaned over and asked him, "Don't they ever feed you at home?" To which this young upstart responded, "But this is *way* better than anything my mom ever makes."

My point exactly, ladies and gentlemen of the jury.

ANTS IN PANTS

Yield: 10 or 12 candies

Who knows what inspired Reese Finer Foods to discontinue its product line of exotic fried and candied insect treats? It couldn't have been from lack of consumer interest: one out of three adults I've asked recalls eating (and, in many instances, enjoying) Reese's chocolate-covered grasshoppers and ants as a kid.

Alas, I've been unable to uncover so much as an empty can from this once-great bug supplier, or even someone who worked for Reese during its heyday. So, in the spirit of entomological entrepreneurship, let's rekindle the lost art (or is it ant?) of making candy with Formicidae.

In this recipe wild ants are frozen, baked in the oven, and then dressed in tantalizing chocolate "pants." A cautionary note: It's easy to "overdress" for the occasion, inadvertently burying the tart flavor of the ants with the rich chocolate coating, so don't be stingy with the insects.

---

8 ounces bittersweet chocolate, chopped

$1/2$ cup (1 stick) butter

1 tablespoon corn syrup

$1/2$ teaspoon Grand Marnier, or orange extract to taste

$1/2$ cup (about 80 to 100) oven-baked western thatching ants or other large-bodied ants (see instructions for Crispy Crickets on page 29)

1. In the top of a double boiler set over hot (but not boiling) water, combine the chocolate, butter, and corn syrup. When the chocolate is melted and the ingredients are evenly blended, stir in the Grand Marnier. Remove from heat and allow the chocolate to cool to 90°F. The chocolate will be shiny and will coat a finger well.

2. Drip small amounts of the melted chocolate mixture on a sheet of foil or parchment paper, forming 10 or 12 disks, each 1 inch in diameter. Quickly pile a spoonful of the baked ants in the center of each circle, then cover with the remaining chocolate. Refrigerate.

3. After the chocolate has set, use a spatula to transfer each chocolate bundle of Ants in Pants to a plate.

Who says nostalgia ain't what it used to be?

PEAR SALAD WITH CHIANGBAI ANTS

Yield: 4 servings

September 7 marks the Feast of Saint Gratus of Aosta, the patron saint of the fear of insects. Among his many miracles, Saint Gratus is said to have aided farmers in the French Alps who vanquished a ravenous swarm of locusts by invoking his name. I chose that significant date to host a five-course bug banquet, a first-of-its-kind feast at Cafe Racer, a charmingly off-kilter drinking and dining establishment on the edge of Seattle's University District. Fifty people paid $20 each to attend this fete and to gorge themselves on Orthopteran Orzo (page 27), Locust Kabobs, a meal-worm-filled *Tenebrio* Terrine, and a sumptuous Pear Salad dotted with Chiangbai Ants. Between courses, the café offered Bug Juice, a non-alcoholic drink, containing cochineal insect dye.

The event was heralded with great enthusiasm by the Seattle media. Writing for the city's alternative newspaper *The Stranger*, Brendan Kiley urged the Cafe Racer team to consider hosting the bug feast more than once a year. He proposed several additional dates, each of them a feast day commemorating other holy men "who specialize in bugs—infestations of, fear of, and bites from": Saint Magnus of Füssen (patron of protection from caterpillars), Saint Narcissus (patron of protection from biting insects), Saint Mawes (patron of protection from *all* insects), and Saint Mark the Evangelist (patron of lawyers).

Chinese ants from the Changbai region are sold commercially as a health supplement in Asia. They reputedly have health benefits, perhaps because of their proximity to the finest ginseng-growing region of China. So if you want to slow the aging process or (to quote the literature) "increase sexual vigor," then these ants are for you.

When I wrote the first edition of this book, there was a local source of dried Chinese black ants in Los Angeles. However, that company no longer sells my ants of choice, opting to carry a line of health-ful ant tinctures instead. As a result, I've had to look for overseas sources, which in my case means begging travelers to the East to bring me back a few vials of China's precious commodity in their luggage.

Without further fanfare, here is the recipe for a tasty salad topped with dried black ants.

3 cups baby spinach, washed and dried

2 crisp pears, peeled, cored, and sliced

$1/2$ cup chopped red bell pepper

2 tablespoons finely chopped shallot

2 tablespoons balsamic vinegar

1 cup shaved Asiago or Parmesan cheese

4 tablespoons dried Changbai ants

1. On four salad plates, arrange the spinach, adding a layer of pear slices to the heap.

2. Sprinkle the bell pepper and shallots over the pears. Splash each salad with about $1/2$ tablespoon of balsamic vinegar.

3. Add the shaved cheese to the salads and sprinkle the ants over the cheese.

4. Feeling antsy? Your salads are now ready to be served.

PART THREE

WHO'S BUGGIN' WHOM?

Nine Ways to Turn the Tables on Household and Garden Pests

Whether gathered from the garden or inside one's home, many pest arthropods make great eating—and they are seldom in short supply. Household pest populations often number in the tens of thousands (no wonder cockroaches are known as "the exterminator's bread and butter"), and the breeding potential of outdoor pests is no less awesome than that of their indoor cousins. Entomologist Glen Herrick has determined that one female cabbage aphid (*Brevicoryne brassicae*) could produce as many as twelve generations during its lifetime, introducing 564 quadrillion (ten to the fifteenth power) offspring—roughly 823 million tons of adult aphids—into one's garden in a year.

Despite their bad reputations, most pest arthropods are really quite clean, devoting considerable time and energy to grooming themselves. If they are washed beforehand and properly prepared, pest bugs pose no greater health risk to diners than do mashed potatoes or other, more socially acceptable fare. However, before cooking with any pest bugs, consider the environment from which these ingredients have been taken. Due to our dependence on insecticides, we have accidentally tainted the flesh of many tasty forms of edible insect life. Even if insecticides are not being used in your garden or home, there's no guarantee that your bugs haven't been accumulating toxic chemicals during nightly visits to your neighbor's place.

For the health-conscious bug eater, it may be best to purchase pest bugs from biological supply houses and other reputable livestock dealers. Cockroaches and other pests from these sources are reared exclusively for laboratory research and classroom study or, in the case of greater wax moth larvae (*Galleria mellonella*) and mealworms (*Tenebrio* sp.), as food for birds, reptiles, and other small animals. These animals are kept in sanitary, toxin-free environments and given specially formulated foods to ensure robustness and rapid growth. By obtaining pests from these sources, bug chefs can guarantee that the meat on their guests' plates—even if it happens to be Cockroach à la King (page 78)—is truly prime.

Even if one can vouch for their upbringing, not all pest arthropods (a list of about two hundred species commonly encountered in the United States alone) are equally appealing. Call me finicky, but I've no desire to try head lice (*Pediculus humanus capitis*), regardless of whether these tiny wingless insects are palatable to the indigenous tribes of the upper Amazon Basin. Nor am I especially interested in captive-bred houseflies (*Musca domestica*), having visited the rearing room of one major supplier and spied the rotting calf's liver on which the fly maggots are cultured. Let's just say that one man's pest is another's repast and leave it at that.

Rustling Up Some Grub

"How can the farmer most successfully battle with the insect devourers of his crops?" mused Vincent Holt, the author of *Why Not Eat Insects?* His suggestion, in case you haven't already guessed: let poor people collect these pests as food.

"Not only would their children then be rewarded by the farmers for hand-picking the destructive insects," noted the nineteenth-century entomophage, "but they would be doubly rewarded by partaking of toothsome and nourishing insect dishes at home." The top candidate among edible pests was the common cockchafer beetle (*Melolontha melolontha*), readily distinguished by Holt because of its grub's "most serviceable size and plumpness."

In Holt's day, common cockchafers were doubly despised because of the damage they inflicted on plants during two separate phases of life. They are no more popular with the farming set today. Underground, cockchafer grubs nibble at the roots of grasses and other plants. When the grubs metamorphose, they emerge from the soil as free-ranging adult beetles that focus their feasting on flowers and foliage. "Literally tooth and nail we ought to battle this enemy, for in both its stages it is a most dainty morsel for the table," Holt urged us.

The choice of cockchafers as food for the nation's needy may have been inspired by an event that took place nearly two centuries before Holt's birth. Writing in the *Philosophical Transactions* in 1697, a Mr. Molineaux told of a time when cockchafer swarms threatened to devour parts of Ireland. So numerous were the pest bugs, claimed Molineaux, that "persons traveling on the roads or abroad in the fields, found it very uneasy to make their way through them, they would so beat and knock themselves against their faces in their flight, and with such a force as to make the place smart and leave a mark behind them." The clouds of cockchafers were a windfall to some, notably swine and poultry, which were more than willing to suffer a few facial bruises in order to fill their bellies with bugs. Dining alongside their livestock were "the poorer sort of the country people," protein-starved citizens of Galway who, observed Molineaux, "had a way of dressing [the dead cockchafers] and living upon them as food."

Make Mine Mopane

Rainfall is scant and the growing season short in the dry brush regions of southern Africa, prompting the female emperor moth (*Gonimbrasia belina*) to make her move in early November, when the buds start to open on the mopane trees. She lays eggs in clusters of two hundred on the young mopane leaves. Shortly after the eggs hatch you can hear the sounds of tiny caterpillar jaws—a noise not unlike light rain—at a respectable distance from the trees.

Feeding on their host plant's leathery but nutritious leaves, these moths-to-be grow rapidly. In less than six weeks they'll grow to more than four inches long and weigh five and a quarter ounces apiece.

Around Christmastime the tree limbs start to bend under the caterpillars' collective weight. This could be interpreted as a sign of trouble, if one were concerned about the mopane trees' health. To rural African women, however, it signals the start of the harvest season. The cash crop, in this case, is not the fruit of the mopane tree but its pest—the emperor moth caterpillars, commonly known as mopane worms.

In a good year mopane worm harvesters may collect up to forty pounds of fat caterpillars in an hour. This bounty is crudely processed: the caterpillars' guts are squeezed out and their bodies briefly boiled in salted water and spread in the sun before the dried worms can be brought to market.

"The end product looks like blackened peanuts, curled and dry and about as palatable as peanut shells to the uninitiated," writes Ellen

Bartlett, a Johannesburg, South Africa–based journalist. Neither the mopane worm's looks nor taste deter regional bug eaters, though, for each dried caterpillar is bursting with digestible protein—as much as 60 percent of the animal's dry weight. Eating twenty of these bugs provides 76 percent of an adult's daily protein requirement and 100 percent of the daily requirement for calcium, phosphorous, riboflavin, and iron.

Until recently the mopane worm biz was fairly small and low-key, with the dried product packaged in small plastic bags or sold by the tin cupful at rural bus stops. Now, however, several large South African firms have picked up the slack, marketing tens of thousands of tons of mopane worms at prices that range from $2 per pound in rural areas to as much as $9 per pound in metropolitan centers. South Africa trades roughly 1.6 million kilos of mopane worms annually, and neighboring Botswana nets an estimated $8 million per year. In Zimbabwe there have even been reports of mopane poaching and stories of armed gangs robbing rural harvesters of their worms.

"The mopane worm will remain a staple," according to Bartlett, "as long as supply can keep pace with demand." In the meantime, there's no better model of environmentally sound pest control than this African form of bug eating.

FOOD FOR THOUGHT

- In northern Italy's Piedmont region and the area around the town of Bergamo, fly maggots are added to rounds of pecorino cheese. Sales of the cheese are prohibited by Italian health authorities, despite its cult following.
- Sixteenth-century physicians prescribed bedbugs in alcohol to be drunk as medicine.
- Lumbermen in early Maine ate carpenter ants, supposedly to prevent scurvy.
- *Popillia femoralis*, a close relative of the pestiferous Japanese beetle (*Popillia japonica*), is considered a delicacy in Cameroon.
- Nearly five pounds of pesticides are applied annually by each of Brazil's twenty-three million farm workers, poisoning an estimated 2 percent of their country's human population.

CHAPTER 6

PREPARING PANTRY PESTS

> 66 Many people still believe that insects are generated spontaneously in grain—probably because most of the insect pests of stored grain are so small that they remain unobserved until they have multiplied to such large numbers that the grain may suddenly seem alive with them. 99 —R. T. Cotton and Wallace Ashby, *Insects: The Yearbook of Agriculture* (1952)

Grain-eating pests are numerous wherever these foods are processed and stored. The remains of one such time-honored freeloader, the red flour beetle, *Tribolium castaneum*, have even been found in alabaster storage vessels from Tutankhamun's tomb. To survive the characteristically moisture-free conditions of grain storage areas, many such pests can get by without so much as a sip of water. They meet their requirements for moisture by extracting water molecules from the carbohydrates in their food.

Chief among these waterless wonders is the mealworm—an aptly named arthropod, at least to my bug-eating comrades and me. The golden-hued larvae of the darkling beetle (*Tenebrio* sp.), mealworms can absorb water vapor from the air even when the relative humidity dips below 50 percent.

Because of their ability to thrive on next to nothing, these protein-rich creatures are ideal bugs for commercial mass production, for consumption by fish, reptiles, amphibians, and birds. Like captive-bred crickets, mealworms have also been embraced by bug-eating attendants of insect fairs and bug fests.

Figures on mealworm sales are truly amazing. On a good day the world's largest dealer, Rainbow Mealworms of Compton, California, ships an estimated three to four million live specimens, meeting the needs of some forty thousand individual and institutional clients. Another of North America's top suppliers, Timberline Live Pet Foods of Marion, Illinois, rears about five hundred million mealworms each year. According to this firm's general manager, Todd Goodman, approximately 60 percent of Timberline's business sales are of so-called "standard" mealworms (*Tenebrio molitor*), glossy inch-long animals that are indistinguishable from the wild infesters of milled cereals and grains. Standard mealworms come in four sizes—mini, small, medium, and large—primarily for sale at pet stores and bait shops in packages of fifty, one hundred, and

five hundred. Bug eaters, however, may prefer to order their mealworms in bulk quantities, priced (as they were in the 1990s, when I began to research this subject) at $7.50 per one thousand mealworms, plus packing and shipping charges.

Rainbow Mealworms, Timberline, and several other suppliers also sell superworms or "king mealworms" (*Zophobas morio*), an entirely different animal. These tropical relatives of temperate pantry pests are more difficult to rear, hence their comparatively higher price (in bulk orders of a thousand, about two cents per mealworm). But the added expense is offset by the superworm's appealingly thin exoskeleton and two-inch-long body—attributes that put these larvae high on the list of edible pests.

Standard mealworms can be housed in a plastic shoebox or other broad-bottomed container with an inch of bran, cornmeal, or oatmeal as bedding. Keep the box in the refrigerator, where the cold temperature will delay the mealworms' development into adult beetles. It's unnecessary to keep a lid on the container, as the box's inhabitants cannot scale the cardboard walls. However, moisture from the refrigerator should not be allowed to drip into the box, which would contaminate the bedding. If you plan on keeping live mealworms for more than a week or two, you'll need to feed them every four or five days. Remove their box from the refrigerator, let it warm to room

NUTRITIONAL ANALYSIS

One standard mealworm contains:
- 20.0 percent protein
- 14.3 percent fat
- 6.7 percent fiber
- 1.3 percent ash
- 61.4 percent moisture

Source: Timberline Live Pet Foods

temperature, and then add a slice of raw carrot or potato. The moist food should be removed and the mealworms returned to the refrigerator after each feeding.

Superworms are more active than ordinary mealworms, a trait that makes them irresistible to pets but may cause some chefs to shudder. They require warmth (between 65°F and 85°F) and should *not* be stored in the refrigerator. They are good climbers, so a container with a tight-fitting lid is imperative. Predisposed to scavenge, superworms need more than grain; a piece of raw carrot, potato, or celery should be included in each container. If the conditions are right, they can live this way for a year and a half without metamorphosing into adult beetles. Watch it, though: Under crowded conditions these larval bugs can turn cannibalistic. Should this happen, your meal is likely to consume itself.

One cup of small "feeder" mealworms contains approximately 2,500 individuals. One cup of superworms contains approximately 250 individuals. Grinding one cup of oven-baked mealworms will produce $1/3$ cup of mealworm flour.

Entomophagy purists avoid cooking with so-called "giant" mealworms. The veal of the edible arthropod world, these specimens of *T. molitor* have been fed growth-regulating

COOKING TIP

To clean mealworms prior to cooking, place a handful in a colander and toss them gently to separate the bugs from any attached food or debris. If you blow across the top of the colander as you do this, any lighter material, including any shed exoskeletons, will waft away. Some chefs use a hair dryer for this purpose. Now pour the mealworms onto a sheet of wax paper. The smooth surface will prevent the live mealworms from crawling away. Discard any dead or dying specimens (these are easy to identify by their darker color and lack of movement), then return the mealworms to the colander, where they can be rinsed with cool water. Pat them dry with a cloth or paper towel. Although some chefs use live mealworms in their recipes, I prefer working with frozen ones that have been thawed. Premeasured quantities of cleaned mealworms can be transferred to zip-top plastic bags and then placed in the freezer for the big sleep.

hormones to keep them forever young. Although they are much larger and plumper than standard mealworms, the purists say they are not nearly as tasty—and they cost twice as much as standard mealworm stock.

Remember that our feathered friends, including sparrows, finches, and many other wild birds, are exceptionally fond of leftovers from mealworm cooking. If you'd like, you can purchase dried mealworms packaged by bird food companies such as Kaytee Pet Products.

> **"** I should not wonder if the silkworm were originally a great plague to gardeners until its real value was discovered, and so it is not utterly impossible that some mode may be found for turning the cockchafer to account. **"** —Reverend J. G. Wood, *Insects at Home* (1873)

COCKROACH À LA KING

Yield: 6 servings

Why not eat roaches, to paraphrase the nineteenth century's Vincent Holt? They're nutritious, delicious, and remarkably easy to obtain.

Admittedly, pest roaches may carry bacteria and viruses, picked up, no doubt, during nightly jaunts to our garbage cans and other less-than-sanitary haunts. However, the same animals reared under laboratory conditions are no germier than the human attendants who care for them.

I purchase my roaches from Carolina Biological Supply in Burlington, North Carolina, where more than twenty thousand of these tasty animals are destined each year for dissection or live study at colleges and universities. The company's catalog lists four different roach species, including my culinary favorite, the American cockroach (*Periplaneta americana*). This particular species is big, with inch-and-a-half-long bodies and leathery, ornately veined wings. They are raised in the company's room-sized "roacharium" and shipped in nifty cylindrical cardboard containers—the kind you'd expect freezer-packed quarts of ice cream to come in. Prior to shipping they've enjoyed something like sixteen square meals a day, partaking of food that's more or less identical to that given mass-cultivated crickets.

To prepare frozen cockroaches for cooking, simply break off the chitin-covered legs, antennae, and both sets of wings. This leaves a bite-sized morsel, about the size of a shelled peanut, that can be left at room temperature to thaw. Save a few intact specimens to garnish your dishes, giving them the added shock value that we entomophagous chefs occasionally seek.

A meal fit for royalty—well, perhaps a deposed prince—this easy but elegant supper proves once again that you don't have to go out to have a good time. Just invite your guests to assist in the preparation of this dish. Or watch their faces at mealtime, as the cooked cockroaches on their plates play hide and seek in the creamy white sauce.

SAUCE

2 cups milk

1 tablespoon butter

$^1/_4$ cup all-purpose flour

1 cup vegetable broth

2 tablespoons butter

36 frozen American cockroaches, thawed

1 cup sliced button mushrooms

1 green bell pepper, sliced

$^1/_4$ cup sherry

Salt and freshly ground pepper to taste

1 pimiento (cherry pepper), cut into thin strips

2 egg yolks

Cooked egg noodles or whole wheat toast for serving

1. To make the sauce, heat the milk and butter in a saucepan over medium heat until the butter has melted. Then add the flour,

combining the ingredients with a wire whisk. Continue whisking until the sauce starts to thicken and then add the vegetable broth. Stir slowly until the sauce is thick and smooth. Remove from the heat and set aside.

2. In a saucepan over medium heat, melt the butter. Add the cockroaches, mushrooms, and bell pepper and sauté until the vegetables are tender, 2 to 3 minutes. Add the cockroach mixture to the pan with the sauce and return to medium heat.

3. Gradually stir in the sherry. Season with salt and pepper to taste.

4. Add the pimiento and simmer until all the ingredients are evenly heated.

5. Shortly before serving, beat the egg yolks and mix with 1 tablespoon warm water. Add the egg yolks to the saucepan. Reduce the heat to low and cook for 1 minute more.

6. Serve the warm cockroach mixture on a bed of cooked egg noodles or whole wheat toast.

Travels with My Ant: Regional Takes on Bug Eating

I'm often asked about the types of people who attend my cooking demonstrations. At the museums, science centers, and schools that I visit, I can usually identify three distinct groups of people. The first bunch is there only to observe. They may be intrigued by the concept of eating bugs, but they aren't quite ready to give it a go. Second are the "I'll try anything once" types. They are open to new experiences and are often into mushroom hunting or interested in foraging other foods from the wild. The third bunch can't wait for me to begin my show. I get the impression that they awakened before dawn and drove in the dark for hours just to be first in line for the deep-fried tarantula legs or a breaded scorpion claw. I appreciate their fervor.

When you travel as much as I do, you get to see how audiences in different parts of the country react to my meals. Californians are my favorites: whenever I ask for volunteer taste testers, a sea of hands will shoot up. New Yorkers are my least favorite: they tend to greet me and my cuisine with the stink eye. Midwesterners are, on average, a conservative lot. There are exceptions, of course. Once I had to ask an audience at Milwaukee's Museum of Natural History to wait until my program was over before helping themselves to the sample cups of Chirpy Chex Party Mix. "People here are really into eating—no matter what it is," the museum's special events planner informed me.

For the most part, I think acceptance or rejection is a reflection of one's prior encounters with arthropods. In New York City, for instance, you're far more likely to bump into cockroaches, flies, and bedbugs than, say, swallowtail butterflies or luna moths. However, if you live in Breaux Bridge, Louisiana, site of the popular Mud Bug (crayfish) Festival, then you might be a bit more accepting of my Scorpion Scaloppine (page 113) or Bugs in a Rug (page 31). St. Bernard School in Breaux Bridge, by the way, is the only place where I've ever run out of bug food during an assembly.

LARVAL LATKES (A.K.A. GRUBSTEAKS)

Yield: 8 servings

I first tried this variation of the traditional northern European dish during Hanukkah. I wanted to see if my friends could tell the difference between mealworms and grated potatoes. They could.

I'm pleased to report, however, that the cheerful orange pancakes with a charming chitinous crunch were quite well received. Some of their success may be attributed to the sour cream and applesauce toppings, which were flavorful complements to the grated onion and yam. The toppings also serve as an edible veil for the insect ingredients. Not everybody wants to see the eight hundred medium-sized standard mealworms that go into this dish.

A word of caution: Neither mealworms nor the darkling beetles into which these creatures metamorphose are kosher, and thus this dish should not be served at gatherings of Orthodox or Conservative Jews.

1 sweet potato
1 small yellow onion
2 large eggs, lightly beaten
$^1/_2$ cup all-purpose flour
$^3/_4$ teaspoon baking powder
Freshly ground pepper to taste
1 cup frozen standard mealworms, thawed
About $^1/_4$ cup peanut oil
Sour cream and/or applesauce for serving (optional)

1. Grate the sweet potato and onion, using a grater with holes that correspond to the size of the mealworms you're using.

2. Combine the sweet potato and onion in a large mixing bowl. Stir in the eggs, flour, baking powder, and pepper.

3. With a wooden spoon, gently stir in the thawed mealworms, taking care not to mash (or otherwise damage) their bodies.

4. In a large skillet, heat $^1/_{16}$ inch of peanut oil over medium-high heat. Fry generous dollops of the batter in the hot oil, cooking them about 2 or 3 minutes per side and gently flattening them with a spatula as they are flipped. As they are finished, drain the latkes on paper towels.

5. Serve immediately, topped with sour cream and/or applesauce or "straight up," as your guests prefer.

CHAPTER 7

GARDEN GRAZERS ALFRESCO

Call it a form of primitive justice, dining on the creatures that routinely devour our vegetables and fruits. Or maybe it's a matter of doing away with the middlemen, as we benefit from the extra protein to be had by moving up a step on the food pyramid.

In the days before DDT and other killer compounds, handpicking was the preferred control method in gardens and farm fields throughout the world. Although extremely labor-intensive, this was (and in many places still is) the only way farmers could effectively reduce the populations of pest insects that fed on their crops. By combining handpicking with intercropping—the wide-spread practice of growing two or more plant species together, with one reducing the probability of insect attack on the other—early agricultural communities could count on consistently high yields.

Today more and more people are adopting the pest control methods of their forebears. In the process, they are discovering the many side benefits of chemical-free living. Unlike with broad-based applications of pesticides, only the targeted pest species are affected by handpicking; bees, butterflies, and many other beneficial land arthropods can escape the deadly clouds of poison. Birds, reptiles, and other creatures that might eat the chemically tainted carcasses are also spared, as are people who expose themselves to pesticides that have leeched into aquifers and other drinking water supplies. It's a win-win situation, for our planet and for us.

When it comes to sweet revenge, there's no better target for reprisal than the tomato hornworm, a voracious marauder of vegetable patches throughout North America. Hornworms (and there are several kinds) are actually caterpillars, not worms. The characteristic horn of this animal might be more accurately called a tail, as it is located on the caterpillar's terminal segment.

Tomato hornworms hatch from tiny greenish-yellow eggs laid on the undersides of leaves. The young pass through a series of molts, reaching maximum size—around four inches—in three or four weeks. With the appetites of high school football players, they chow down on our precious greenery, robbing not just our tomatoes but also our eggplants, peppers, and potato plants of their leaves.

Full-grown hornworm caterpillars burrow several inches into the soil and pupate, resting quietly inside dull brownish cocoons. If the conditions are right, they may emerge after two to four weeks; more often than not, however, they stay buried until spring. The emerging moths (whopping five-inchers variously referred to as hummingbird or sphinx moths) make their way to the soil surface before they deposit eggs on tomato plants, starting the cycle all over again.

Travels with My Ant: Health Department High Jinks

What do health inspectors think of my bugs? In general, they've been easy to deal with, and I must say that I appreciate their efforts to keep us safe. But over the past fifteen years I've had a handful of strange run-ins.

In the spring of 2000 I was hired by the USA Network to help promote *They Nest*, a made-for-TV movie about a village in Maine that's besieged by an army of carnivorous African cockroaches. To introduce the film to its target audience—guys in their twenties—the USA Network decided to host a series of cockroach-eating contests. Mobile kitchens would be erected outside Wrigley Field in Chicago, Yankee Stadium in the Bronx, Safeco Field in Seattle, and Boston's Fenway Park. The first contestant at each location to finish a plateful of twenty oven-baked cockroaches would win a $10,000 prize. (Alas, the second prize was a USA Network T-shirt.)

The tour's arrangers contacted the health departments of each city we'd be visiting, asking what, if any, permits we'd need to obtain. In New York and Chicago the city's health inspectors barely batted an eye, but in Boston they pitched a fit, flatly refusing to sanction our bug-eating event.

So, yes, I was banned in Boston, just like Henry Miller's *Tropic of Cancer*. When the time came for me to unveil some of my entrées outside Fenway Park, I had to tell the crowd that, in accordance with their health department's decree, I could not legally serve any of the dishes I had just prepared.

"However, I can't stop you from helping yourselves," I told the onlookers. Many people did.

My dealings with the health department in my hometown, Seattle, on that trip were nearly as frustrating. When reviewing our permit request, one civil servant told us that if I'd be cooking outdoors, we'd need to erect a canopy—"to keep any flying insects from falling into the food."

WASABI WAX WORMS

Yield: 4 servings

I first met with San Franciscan Daniella Martin in the winter of 2008 at a Starbucks near my home. The topic of our coffee klatch? Edible bugs, of course. Shortly thereafter she launched the first of her popular videos on her website *Girl Meets Bug*. It showed the fledgling entomophage in her home kitchen making and tasting her new creation, wax worm tacos.

Since then Daniella has carved a niche for herself as an outspoken promoter of insect eating for the sake of our planet. And she does so through personal appearances and an active online presence in a way that's appealing and fun.

The recipe that Daniella contributed here is for an innovative yet unassuming appetizer. A harmonious blend of sweet, salty, and spicy flavors, it hints at her earlier career when she assisted a master chef at a sushi establishment.

"Don't worry if you hear popping sounds coming from the oven," she explained to me in an email. "It's just the frozen wax worms snapping up off the baking sheet—a sign that they'll be ready to go soon."

$^1/_2$ cup (approximately 250) frozen wax worms
$^1/_2$ teaspoon light brown sugar
$^1/_4$ teaspoon salt
Wasabi powder to taste

1. Preheat the oven to 350°F.
2. Spread the frozen wax worms on a lightly oiled baking sheet and bake until crispy and golden, 10 to 12 minutes.
3. Transfer the wax worms to a wok or 10-inch skillet. Place over medium heat, add the brown sugar and salt, and cook, tossing with a spatula or wooden spoon, until the sugar begins to caramelize. Add the wasabi powder and cook, stirring, for 30 seconds.
4. Transfer the wasabi-glazed wax worms to a shallow serving bowl and let cool before sharing with guests.

COOKING TIP

Many wax worm suppliers ship their stock in shredded newspaper or wood shavings. Because the larvae don't eat these media, there's no need to purge the animals before cooking with them. Just empty the container onto a cookie sheet and, with your bare hands or bamboo tongs, pick out the larvae. Then rinse the ingredients, pat them dry, and freeze them for later use.

SUPERWORM TEMPURA WITH PLUM DIPPING SAUCE

Yield: 4 servings

The hardest part of this recipe is figuring out which end of a superworm is its head. Seriously though, the only real challenge is finding a source of umeboshi, the Japanese pickled plums that give the dipping sauce its piquant flavoring. Puréed umeboshi (called *bainiku*) can be used as a substitute, but this, too, is not often found at the corner store.

Most Asian groceries, however, as well as many specialty food shops, carry one or both ingredients. Umeboshi is a common ingredient in Japanese cuisine, so you probably won't have to explain to most clerks at Asian grocery stores what you're using the stuff for—which is a good thing. Although many different kinds of insect are considered delicacies in Japan, including *sangi* (the fried pupae of the silk moth, *Bombyx mori*) and *hachi-no-ko* (the boiled larvae of the *Vespula* wasp), mealworm tempura has yet to take hold.

And while we're on the subject of taking hold, this recipe calls for the chef to manipulate a minimum of two dozen superworms, one at a time—an act that is time-consuming and a bit disconcerting for the inexperienced superworm handler. Because of this, this dish makes a better appetizer than a main course. If you are loathe to touch the mealworms with your bare hands, try using a pair of long bamboo tongs, which are much gentler on the bugs than metal tweezers.

If you still haven't found your superworm's head, it's the first of thirteen bead-sized body segments. The second, third, and fourth segments each sport one pair of stubby little legs. The next eight are graced with spiracles, the openings to tiny air tubes, through which the larvae breathe. The terminal segment (number thirteen) lacks spiracles but contains many small sensory hairs. Congratulations: You've now completed the coursework for Superworm 101.

DIPPING SAUCE

6 tablespoons rice vinegar

1/4 cup firmly packed brown sugar

1 umeboshi (preserved sour) plum, broken into pieces, or 1 teaspoon bainiku paste

1 small red chile, finely chopped

BATTER

1 medium egg

1/2 cup cold water

1/2 cup all-purpose flour

1/2 teaspoon baking soda

24 frozen superworms, defrosted

2 cups peanut oil

1. To make the dipping sauce, combine the vinegar and brown sugar in a small saucepan and heat until the sugar dissolves. Add the umeboshi plum to the saucepan and cook, stirring for 8 to 10 minutes, until the mixture thickens.

2. Add the chopped chile, stir, and remove the pan from the heat. Let cool, then pour the cooled sauce into 4 small bowls. Set aside.

3. Rinse the superworms, pat dry, and set aside.

4. To make the batter, beat the egg in a small mixing bowl until smooth. Slowly add the cold water, continuing to beat until evenly mixed. Add the flour and baking soda and beat gently until combined; the batter should be a bit lumpy.

5. Let the batter sit at room temperature while heating the peanut oil over high heat until hot but not smoking in a frying pan or wok.

6. Grasping each superworm by the head, dip three-fourths of its body into the batter. The body should be lightly coated; any excess batter can be shed by gently running the superworm across the lip of the bowl.

7. Drop the battered superworms into the hot peanut oil. With a slotted spoon, turn each superworm once or twice. As they heat up, the worms' bodies will expand, causing the unbattered portions to elongate. As soon as the batter turns golden and crisp, about 30 seconds, remove the worms. Leaving the worms in the oil for too long may cause their bodies to burst, venting any built-up steam and possibly splashing you with hot oil in the process.

8. Drain the fried superworms on paper towels, then transfer them to a serving plate. Serve warm with the dipping sauce alongside.

ENTO-EPHEMERA

What do we mean when we call something a pest? Basically, that it's unwanted or in the way. Telephone solicitors at suppertime are pests. So are arthropods that don't know their place. A single pest is seldom a problem. Most of us can live with one cutworm or a single sales call. Unfortunately, in either instance there's no such thing.

FRIED GREEN TOMATO HORNWORMS

Yield: 8 servings

What does a tomato hornworm taste like? Well, what would you taste like if you'd been stuffing yourself solely with tomato leaves for the better part of a month? Hornworms, which are ridiculously rich in chlorophyll, taste great with just about any summer vegetable, but my favorite recipe draws inspiration from the cuisine of the Whistle Stop Café, that fictitious Alabama diner made famous by novelist Fannie Flagg.

"You'll think you died and gone to heaven," boasts Flagg of her recipe for fried green tomatoes, to which I add, if you *do* go to heaven, please ask the powers that be to watch over the tomato hornworms in my vegetable patch.

---

3 tablespoons olive oil

32 tomato hornworms

4 medium green tomatoes, sliced into sixteen $1/4$-inch rounds

Salt and freshly ground pepper to taste

White cornmeal

16 to 20 small basil leaves

HARVESTING HINT

On a good day you can collect ten to twenty gargantuan hornworm caterpillars from an average-sized tomato patch. Take the culprits inside and refrain from feeding them, allowing these bugs to purge themselves of any tomato leaves they've eaten. Or try introducing another food, such as basil, that will actually make these ingredients even tastier. After two days, wash them under the tap, then throw them into plastic bags and store in your freezer for future food use.

1. In a large skillet or wok, heat 1 tablespoon of oil over medium-high heat. Add the hornworms and fry lightly for about 4 minutes, taking care not to rupture the cuticles of each insect under high heat. Remove with a slotted spoon and set aside.

2. Season the tomato rounds with salt and pepper to taste, then coat with cornmeal on both sides.

3. In another large skillet or wok, heat the remaining oil and fry the tomatoes until lightly browned on both sides.

4. Top each tomato round with 2 fried tomato hornworms.

5. Garnish with basil leaves and serve immediately.

PIZ-ZZ-ZZ-ZA

Yield: 4 servings

Periodical cicadas are the Rip Van Winkles of the insect world. The young of six North American species spend most of their lives underground, seemingly dead to the world as the seasons pass by. But, after a whopping thirteen to seventeen years (depending on the species), they are prompted by some subtle cue to climb out of their lairs en masse. All at once the landscape is full of savory morsels—the wingless, soft-bodied subadults—which often number in the thousands. A feast in the making for the enterprising entomophage!

But how to prepare these long-awaited insect treats? Members of the Onondaga tribe of north-eastern North America roasted them in a pot without water, adding a little animal fat to the final mix. The former chief of the U.S. Department of Agriculture's entomology division, Leland O. Howard, ate them in a plain stew, a thick milk stew, and broiled. "The most palatable method of cooking is to fry in batter, when they remind one of shrimps," he wrote in 1885.

Periodical cicadas should be harvested immediately after they have undergone their final molt—usually within minutes of their appearance above ground. Clinging by their claws to the bark of trees, these freshly formed adults have yet to develop fully functional wings. As such, they are sitting ducks, easily captured by hand or with a small net. To arrest any further development, we recommend plunging these captives into ice water (as Leland Howard did) or freezing them. Otherwise you may have to mount an aerial search to recapture your ingredients.

Years back, when I suddenly found myself up to my elbows in *Magicicada cassini,* also known as Cassin's seventeen-year cicada, I took the advice of University of Chicago professor emeritus Monte Lloyd. His suggestion—to prepare the catch as a topping for pizza—was an immediate hit in my kitchen. I can't wait for the next major emergence of this delicious substitute for sliced andouille sausage, some time in the summer of 2024.

DOUGH

1 teaspoon active dried yeast

1 teaspoon sugar

$^3/_4$ cup warm water

1 tablespoon olive oil

$2^1/_4$ cups bread flour

$^1/_3$ cup cornmeal

TOMATO SAUCE

2 tablespoons olive oil

1 yellow onion, finely chopped

1 clove garlic, crushed

1 pound tomatoes, peeled and sliced into $^3/_4$-inch chunks

1 tablespoon tomato paste

$^1/_2$ teaspoon sugar

$^1/_2$ teaspoon chopped fresh oregano

$^1/_2$ teaspoon chopped fresh basil

Salt and freshly ground pepper to taste

TOPPINGS

$^{1}/_{2}$ cup grated mozzarella cheese

8 sundried tomatoes in oil

6 marinated artichoke hearts

8 subadult periodical cicadas, thawed frozen or freshly caught, or 40 Crispy Crickets (page 29)

1 teaspoon red pepper flakes

1. To make the dough, in a small bowl, combine the yeast, sugar, and $^{1}/_{4}$ cup of the water. In a large bowl, combine the yeast mixture with the olive oil, the remaining $^{1}/_{2}$ cup water, the flour, and cornmeal. Mix to form a soft dough, then knead on a lightly floured board until smooth and elastic, about 10 minutes.

2. Place the dough in a greased bowl and cover with a cloth or plastic wrap. Let rise until doubled in size, about 45 minutes.

3. While waiting for the dough to rise, begin making the tomato sauce. Heat the olive oil in a medium saucepan and medium-high heat. Add onion and garlic and sauté until soft.

4. Stir in tomatoes, tomato paste, sugar, oregano, and basil. Season with salt and pepper to taste. Cover the saucepan and simmer for 30 minutes, stirring occasionally. Remove from the heat.

5. Punch down the risen dough and knead briefly. Place in the center of an oiled 12-inch pizza pan. Using your knuckles, press outward until the dough is evenly spread, filling the pan. Pinch a lip around the edge to contain the sauce. Brush the dough with olive oil.

6. Preheat the oven to 425°F.

7. Spoon the tomato sauce over the dough. Spread the mozzarella uniformly over the sauce.

8. Drain the sundried tomatoes, reserving the oil. Coarsely chop the sundried tomatoes and the artichoke hearts, then artfully arrange the two items over the cheese. Top the pizza with the cicadas.

9. Sprinkle the pizza with 1 or 2 tablespoons of the reserved oil from the sundried tomatoes. Bake until the cheese has melted and dough is crisp and golden, 15 to 20 minutes. Dust with the red pepper flakes and serve.

10. Wait 13 to 17 years and repeat this entire sequence.

PEST-O

I wondered what to do with the rice weevils (*Sitophilus oryzae*) I'd occasionally find in my canisters. At around three millimeters in length, they're way too small to base a meal around, and I've never found them or their outdoor-dwelling cousins in sufficient quantities to warrant concocting a dish.

Then I met Sharon Collman, a Washington State University entomologist, then working on her master's degree in, you guessed it, weevil-ology. She generously offered to share a few dozen of her research specimens, provided she got a prominent plug in my cookbook.

"Look at one of these guys under a scanning electron microscope," Sharon told me, "and you'll see that its body is pockmarked with tiny pits." Sticking straight up from the pits are small hairs, called sensilla. Each hair is remarkably sensitive to external stimuli, including subtle vibrations.

Because wood weevils are so highly aware, they can get the jump on any predators. When alarmed, says Sharon, they draw in their legs and antennae and "play possum," falling to the ground and remaining motionless until they're certain the threat has passed.

This makes collecting weevils a snap. Just go out into your garden with a sheet of cardboard. Hold the cardboard underneath just about any plant (weevils aren't particular) and give the plant a shake. As they drop off, the hard-bodied weevils make a loud rapping noise on the cardboard. Even on a moonless night you can count the taps and tell how many weevils you just caught.

On an average night of foraging in her backyard Sharon finds a few weevils, but occasionally she finds a "bingo plant," from which a shower of thirty or forty can be nabbed. Depending on conditions in your garden, it could be quite easy to make my version of a classic Genoese delicacy.

---

36 oven-roasted root weevils or other weevil species (see instructions for Crispy Crickets on page 29)

2 cups fresh basil leaves, washed and patted dry

2 cloves garlic, peeled

1 cup walnuts

$^3/_4$ cup chopped fresh parsley

$^1/_2$ cup olive oil

1 cup grated Parmesan cheese

$^1/_4$ cup grated pecorino Romano cheese

3 tablespoons butter, softened

Salt and freshly ground pepper to taste

1. Using a mortar and pestle, pulverize the dried weevils.

2. Combine the basil, garlic, walnuts, parsley, and olive oil in a food processor or blender. Slowly blend to a smooth paste.

3. Pour the paste into a bowl and beat in the two grated cheeses and pulverized weevils by hand.

4. When the cheeses and weevils are well mixed, beat in the softened butter.

5. Season with salt and pepper to taste.

6. Before spooning the pesto over pasta, stir in a tablespoon of the hot water in which the pasta was boiled.

ALPHA-BAIT SOUP

Yield: 4 servings

I wonder what my former bee-keeping neighbor, Les, would think if he knew I'd been rearing the larvae of greater wax moths (*Galleria mellonella*). For umpteen years he's taken extreme measures to keep these animals away from his hives. Once introduced in a hive, the pudgy white larvae tunnel into the comb, fouling the honey while feeding on the beeswax that contains it.

Healthy bee colonies can defend themselves against such depredations, with worker bees hauling the larvae, commonly known as wax worms, and any egg-laying adult wax moths out of the hive before much damage can be done. However colonies that are already in decline can be pushed over the edge, especially in the fall, when the moths have reared multiple broods. Because a single wax moth can lay between six hundred and a thousand eggs at a time, it's inevitable that their offspring will eventually outnumber their hymenopteran hosts.

Few arthropods are as inherently delicious as these potentially pestiferous piffles. In the past, they have been used as bait for catching freshwater game fish or to feed pet reptiles and amphibians. But a few people have been extolling the wax worm's food value. In his 1976 book *Entertaining with Insects*, Ronald Taylor wrote, "They are our favorite insect . . . thin skinned, tender and succulent. . . . If only they were commercially available, we would have centered most of our recipes around them."

I, too, am enamored of wax worms and have made it my mission to locate reliable sources of these subtle almond-flavored delicacies. In the years since Taylor's book was published, several large-scale rearing operations have sprung up, making wax worms as accessible year-round as live crickets and mealworms. (A list of reputable wax worm dealers is contained in the Resources section.)

2 tablespoons vegetable oil
1 clove garlic, minced
1 medium yellow onion, diced
1 red or green bell pepper, diced
1 stalk celery, cut into $1/2$-inch pieces
1 large tomato, cored and diced
2 cups vegetable broth
$3/4$ cup cooked pinto beans
2 tablespoons tomato paste
$1^1/_2$ teaspoons dried oregano
Salt and freshly ground pepper to taste
50 frozen wax worms, thawed
Fresh-baked bread for serving

1. In a stockpot over medium-high heat, warm the oil. Add the garlic, onion, and vegetables and sauté until the vegetables are tender, about 6 to 8 minutes.

2. Add vegetable broth, beans, tomato paste, oregano, and salt and pepper to taste. Reduce the heat to medium-low and simmer for 45 minutes, stirring occasionally.

3. Add the wax worms and simmer for another 10 minutes.

4. Ladle into soup bowls and serve with bread. Like trout and bluegill, your guests will be hooked on wax worms.

WHITE CHOCOLATE AND WAX WORM COOKIES

Yield: about 3 dozen cookies

These are likely the best bug cookies you'll ever eat. And if your granny couldn't see the baked caterpillars peeking out of the dough, she'd undoubtedly ask for seconds.

I bring these treats, which are sure conversation starters, when I'm asked to appear on radio talk shows. If I'm successful, after the banter has subsided, listeners will hear the sighs of contentment from the on-air hosts. Trust me on this: they're *that* good.

When baked, those chubby ivory-colored caterpillars taste like pistachios. What's not to like? Based on flavor alone, Julia Child would have endorsed this recipe—and probably asked for seconds or thirds.

$1^2/_3$ cups all-purpose flour
$^3/_4$ teaspoon baking powder
$^1/_2$ teaspoon baking soda
$^1/_2$ teaspoon salt
$^3/_4$ cup butter, softened
$^3/_4$ cup firmly packed brown sugar
$^1/_3$ cup granulated sugar
1 teaspoon vanilla extract
1 large egg
2 cups white chocolate chunks or morsels
$^3/_4$ cup (about 375) frozen wax worms, thawed

1. Preheat the oven to 375°F.

2. In a small bowl, combine the flour, baking powder, baking soda, and salt. In a large mixing bowl, beat together the butter, brown and granulated sugars, and vanilla extract until creamy.

3. Stir the egg into the butter mixture, then gradually beat in the flour mixture. Stir in the white chocolate chunks and half of the wax worms, reserving the rest for garnishing the cookies.

4. Drop the batter by rounded teaspoonful onto nonstick baking sheets.

5. Gently press 2 or 3 of the remaining wax worms into the top of each cookie.

6. Bake until the edges of each cookie are lightly browned, 8 to 12 minutes.

7. Let cookies cool on the baking sheets for 2 minutes, then transfer them to a wire rack to cool completely.

" Anyone who enjoys the flavor of potato chips, corn puffs, or the like would delight in the taste of fried wax moth larvae. We can imagine them fried . . . salted, packaged in cellophane, and displayed in supermarkets alongside the other snack items."
—Ronald Taylor and Barbara Carter, *Entertaining with Insects*

PART FOUR

SIDE ORDERS

A Smorgasbord of Treats from Assorted Arthropod Taxa

Imagine a restaurant that served every kind of bug. The menu for such an establishment would be as thick as the Midtown Manhattan telephone directory, with the names and prices of at least 1.5 million entrées spread across its pages.

This number—1.5 million—may actually be a low estimate of species diversity among the land arthropods. After surveying invertebrates in the treetops of the South American rain forest, one entomologist with the Smithsonian Institution in Washington, D.C., suggested that the real number should be more like thirty million—and this just for insects. Reserving several thousand extra pages for the species of centipedes, millipedes, scorpions, spiders, and such, the restaurant's menu would more closely resemble the phone books of London, Tokyo, and Los Angeles strapped together.

As I pointed out in this book's introduction, not every bug is edible. However, for the sake of discussion, let's assume that one in a thousand is. Based on the high estimate of species abundance, there could be some thirty thousand arthropods from which to pick and choose. With the low estimate, there would still be around 1,500—enough for you to order a different bug dish every day for four years!

The number of species that are intentionally brought to the table worldwide is much smaller than this. Ronald Taylor describes about 250 species in his book *Butterflies in My Stomach*, and Taylor's principle source, Bodenheimer's *Insects as Human Food*, only identifies one or two dozen more. In both books the majority of edible bugs belong to the insect orders Coleoptera (beetles), Orthoptera (grasshoppers and their kin), or Hymenoptera (ants, bees, et cetera). The rest are a mixed bag of bugs that includes the dragonflies (order Odonata), luna moths (order Lepidoptera), giant centipedes (order Scolopendromorpha), wolf spiders (order Arachnida), and water bugs (order Hemiptera—remember, the "true" bugs?). It's now time for these animals to walk onto the frying pan and into the fire for this, the concluding section of this book.

CHAPTER 8

SPINELESS DELIGHTS

What makes one arthropod so appealing and another so appalling? In general, our food preferences vary widely from one culture to the next, rendering it impossible to make any blanket statements about them. However, it's safe to say that all edible arthropods share certain attributes, traits that have made them honored guests at bug banquets throughout the world.

The first and foremost trait is availability. Most edible bugs are collectible throughout the year, especially in tropical regions, where land arthropods are so numerous that the supply almost always exceeds the demand. In colder, less nurturing climes bugs may be seasonally abundant. These animals have learned to make hay while the sun is shining, so to speak, in the few good months of the year. In turn, people from these same regions make the most out of the insects, stockpiling them for rationed consumption.

A second commonality among edible arthropods is what my friends in the commercial fishing industry call the catch per unit effort, or CPUE. If it takes three weeks of hard work to collect one kind of bug from which to cook a meal, then the CPUE for that species would be pathetically low (and a cuisine based on that species would be slimming at best). Alternatively, if one can stand in a spot and, within an hour or two, fill a few baskets with bugs, then the CPUE would be vastly improved (as would the chances of getting a bank to finance your new bug-processing plant).

Third, edible bugs must be pleasing to the palate, at least to the people who have collected them. Admittedly, there are many places where people eat bugs primarily for the protein that they offer and where palatability is less of a concern. However, even among these societies, insects and other arthropods are gobbled with great gusto—suggesting that although certain bugs may be an acquired taste, the act of bug eating is not solely motivated by hunger.

Healing Bugs of Yore

"Take two pill bugs and call me in the morning." This advice could very well have come from a medieval physician prescribing the cure for any number of ills. The medicine chest of such a healer might contain dried cicadas, roasted grasshoppers, and *spiritus formicarium* (crushed ants in alcohol), all of which were thought to have strong curative powers.

An array of bug-based remedies is contained in *De methodo medendi* by Galen, an esteemed doctor of medicine from the second century. Many of Galen's cures were rehashed for hundreds of years thereafter. (My favorite of his remedies—"If the swoln breasts do feel great pain, smeer them with Earth-worms, 'twill help them amain"—is reprinted in Mouffet's *The Theater of Insects* from 1658.)

Much excitement, medical and otherwise, was and continues to be focused on the European blister beetle (*Lytta vesicatoria*), from which the legendary extract Spanish fly is obtained. The extract is a powerful irritant to human skin, hence the source insect's common name.

During the reign of Germany's Frederick the Great, blister beetle secretions (called cantharides) were prescribed as a cure for hydrophobia. According to Lucy W. Clausen,

author of *Insect Fact and Folklore*, the top-secret German formula called for "twenty-five beetles that had been preserved in honey, two drachms of powdered black ebony, one drachm of Virginia snakeroot, and one ditto of lead filings, twenty-five grains of fungus Sorbi to be reduced to a very fine substance; the whole, with two ounces of theriaca of Venice (and if necessary, a little elder-root) to be formed into an electuary." For this remedy to work, says Clausen, the beetles had to be captured with a noose of human hair around their necks, then hung out to dry on the same slender strand.

Even Pliny knew about the Spanish fly bug. The Greek scholar claimed that merely holding one of the metallic blue beetles was enough to stimulate the bladder. To a degree, Pliny was right; when absorbed into the bloodstream, the active ingredient in the beetles' secretions can irritate the kidneys and other internal organs. In the eighteenth century rumors started circulating that cantharides could also inflame the reproductive tracts of both men and women, arousing both

ENTO-EPHEMERA

A professor at the National Autonomous University in Mexico City and author of *Creepy Crawly Cuisine: The Gourmet Guide to Edible Insects,* Dr. Julieta Ramos Elorduy has compiled a list of more than one hundred species of insects that are eaten in various parts of her country.

> "Etymologically speaking, the word 'medicine' has entomological roots—it derives from the same root as does the word 'mead,' or fermented honey wine, to which were ascribed remarkable curative powers." —May Berenbaum, *Bugs in the System: Insects and Their Impact on Human Affairs*

sexes to wanton acts of passion. Somehow, however, the extreme toxicity of cantharides was overlooked—at least until 1772, when the nefarious Marquis de Sade was arrested and tried in Marseilles for poisoning several prostitutes while endeavoring to excite them with the bug-based love potion.

Should you still care to experiment with blister beetle by-products, Clausen offers detailed instructions on how to brew up a batch:

> To kill and preserve the blister beetles as quickly as possible, before they exude any of their valuable secretion, the beetles are plunged into vinegar diluted with water, or else placed in sieves and exposed to the fumes of vinegar, ammonia chloroform, burning sulphur or carbon bisulfide. . . . They are next dried naturally in the sun, or in specially built ovens. When dried the beetles are stored in casks, which are sealed to exclude as much atmospheric moisture as possible.

The curative powers of edible arthropods have been recognized by Asians for many centuries. Several insect-related remedies are cited in the 168-volume *Prescriptions for Universal Relief*, published during the Ming dynasty (1368–1644). Traditional wisdom from this weighty tome is still heeded today. Visit an apothecary in the heart of San Francisco's Chinatown and you're certain to find dried

cockroaches, blister beetles, praying mantids, and cicadas in stock.

Particularly prized for its powers against tetanus and hepatitis is *wu kung*, a centipede collected near the watercourses of Suzhou, south of China's Yangtze River. Before *wu kung* can be ingested, this healing bug is stripped of its limbs, roasted, and pulverized, then mixed with cow's milk. Just as effective against an array of ailments is *pai chiang t'san,* bleached silkworms that have been obtained in the Yinhuan district of China during the fourth moon. These minute helpers are fire-dried, powdered, and mixed with juice from fresh gingerroot—a concoction that may be more palatable than silkworm excrement straight up—and are purported by the Chinese to be an effective treatment for typhus and stomach troubles.

GIANT WATER BUG ON WATERCRESS

Yield: 4 servings of 2 bugs each

My first opportunity to eat bugs took place more than three decades ago in Nakhon Pathom, Thailand, home of the fabulous "Mother Temple," Phra Pathom Chedi, billed as the tallest Buddhist monument in the world. Each year in November, as part of the region's big county fair, the temple's terraced grounds are taken over by a tent city of vendor's stalls, at which sellers of everything from fancy goldfish to religious amulets vie for the fairgoers' loot. Ringing this circle of sellers and buyers are numerous food stalls where a variety of festive finger foods, some appetizing, others eyebrow raising by Western standards, can be bought.

At one of these food stands, next to a cheery display of fried chicken feet, I saw my first edible arthropods: three-inch-long members of the family Belostomatidae, giant water bugs being sold as carryout snacks.

I don't recall the price of these odd-looking comestibles, but I still have a vivid mental picture of the triangular heads, brown visorlike eyes, and sharply pointed raptorial forelegs that are the identifying characteristics of one of the largest bugs on our planet.

I lacked the courage to try either the chicken's feet or the giant water bugs. Over the years, however, I've had plenty of time to familiarize myself with giant water bugs and to kick myself for not seizing the opportunity to sample Southeast Asia's biggest, and perhaps tastiest, native bug.

I've since learned that what I saw were probably specimens of *Lethocerus indicus*, a common inhabitant of Southeast Asia's many freshwater rivers, streams, and canals. As their name implies, all water bugs are aquatic, living almost all of their adult lives in the drink. Yet they do step out of the tub each spring in order to colonize other water bodies in the rice-growing plains. It is during this airborne phase that they are commonly collected and brought to markets at Nakhon Pathom and elsewhere.

Believe it or not, Thailand's giant water bugs are a far cry from being the largest of their kind: one South American species is about four inches long. North America's belostomatids are nowhere near this gigantic, but many of the continent's nineteen recognized species are still more than a mouthful. My favorite, *Lethocerus americanus*, is both big and abundant, easily plucked from slow-moving rural creeks and streams across the United States.

Many species of giant water bugs are attracted to bright lights, a fact that makes harvesting belostomatids a snap. Simply hang a lantern at the water's edge and, as night falls, scoop up any and all comers. The live animals should be handled carefully, as they are capable of giving a nasty bite—no doubt the inspiration for the their colorful nickname, the toe-biter.

By capturing water bugs in this way, I've not only been given a second chance to sample *maeng dana*, as this treat is called in Thailand, but I've also been able to make my own *nam prik mangda*, a spicy Thai condiment made by mashing the beetles and mixing them with sugar, garlic, shallots, *nam pla* (fish sauce), and hot peppers.

The preparation of traditional *maeng dana* is simple: whole giant water bugs are boiled and then lightly sprinkled with salt before they are served. In my slightly more elaborate recipe, the cooked insects are spread on a bed of watercress (an homage to their aquatic habitat) and topped with a light ginger sauce, a subtly sweet complement to the giant water bug's somewhat earthy taste.

8 frozen adult Lethocerus water bugs, thawed

2 bunches watercress, washed and trimmed

SAUCE

3 tablespoons rice vinegar

3 tablespoons sugar

6 tablespoons water

2 tablespoons light soy sauce

1 teaspoon cornstarch

2 teaspoons finely minced fresh ginger

1. Bring 2 quarts of lightly salted water to a boil. Add the water bugs and return to a boil. Remove the water bugs after 2 minutes, pat dry, and set aside.

2. To make the sauce, combine the rice vinegar, sugar, water, and 1 tablespoon of the soy sauce in a small saucepan over high heat. Bring to a boil, reduce the heat to low, and simmer for 5 minutes, stirring occasionally.

3. In a small bowl, combine the cornstarch and the remaining 1 tablespoon soy sauce. Stir this into the sauce and simmer until slightly thickened.

4. Remove the saucepan from the heat and stir in the ginger. Let stand for 1 or 2 minutes.

5. Mound the watercress on the center of a platter or large plate. Make a ring of water beetles in the center of the mound. Dribble the slightly cooled ginger sauce over the beetles.

As they say in Thailand, *Chuen lui, krap.* In other words, "Please, enjoy this dish."

COOKING TIP

At many Asian grocery stores you can purchase a slightly bitter substance in an alcohol solution labeled Mangdana Essence. Its ingredients are listed as "10 percent synthetic fine aromatics," plus ethyl heptanoate, hexenyl acetate, hexenyl hexanoate, and hexenol—in other words, the constituents of the giant water bug's paired basal glands. Add a few drops of this discreetly labeled product to store-bought sauces from Thailand or Vietnam for extra authenticity.

WATERMELON AND WATER BUG SURPRISE

Yield: 4 servings of 3 cubes each

This recipe is my take on one developed by Dave Gracer, founder of SmallStock Food Strategies. An empassioned entomophage, Dave is a master at amassing exotic food insects and their relatives. The inventory of his Providence, Rhode Island, company varies from month to month. "When I can get katydids from Texas, scorpions from China, or mopane worms from Zambia or South Africa, it's wonderful," he tells me. "But those shipments are often nonrenewable, and when they're gone, there's little I can do except hustle for other sources and opportunities."

Suffice it to say, Dave has an inside track on bug suppliers—and sometimes that track leads no further than to a nearby grocery store. During our first face-to-face encounter, which took place after one of my cooking demos at the Roger Williams Park Zoo, Dave escorted me to an Asian grocer a few miles away. Here he whisked me through the small shop to the frozen food section, where the store kept its trove of giant water bugs, imported from Thailand and packaged two to a shrink-wrapped package.

I purchased a two-pack and hand-carried it back to Seattle, where a friend skillfully pinned the bugs to a sheet of cardboard to make a pair of mounted trophies that remind me of my auspicious meeting with Mr. G. I've since purchased Cambodian mole crickets, winged leafcutter ants, and a few other hard-to-obtain delicacies from SmallStock Food Strategies' larder.

By his own admission, Dave is more of a food assembler than a chef. To create his dish he worked with Chef Branden Lewis, then the chef instructor at the Genesis Center of Providence, to develop a recipe with visual as well as gustatory pizzazz. Dave writes of this recipe, "The meat is intensely flavorful and aromatic; the saltiness comes through on a wave of fruity and flowery notes. The experience is altogether startling and pairs well with the other ingredients."

I couldn't have said it better. Here's my take on Branden and Dave's recipe.

---

4 giant water bugs

1 Granny Smith apple, cut into 12 wedges

12 watermelon cubes, each $1^1/_2$ inches across

Juice of 1 lemon

4 sprigs of mint

4 paper cocktail parasols (optional)

1. If the water bugs are preserved in salt, rinse them in cold water. Bring a small saucepan of water to a boil and briefly blanch the water bugs for about 1 minute. Drain and set aside.

continued

2. Place an apple wedge on top of each watermelon cube and coat each apple wedge with a dash of lemon juice to keep it from turning brown before serving.

3. Place a water bug on its back, with its legs facing you and its head pointing downward, and grasp the body firmly between thumb and forefinger. Using a small, sharp knife, pierce the center of the water bug's thorax, extending the cut downward. Twist the knife slightly to fully break the chest plate.

4. Remove the knife and place both of your thumbnails in the incision, folding the insect open by cracking the dorsal plate. This will reveal the meat in the thorax.

5. Use a grapefruit spoon to scoop out the meat. Divide the meat into three portions. Put each portion on top of an apple wedge.

6. Repeat with the remaining water bugs, watermelon cubes, and apple slices. Put the completed treats on a platter or small plates.

7. Add sprigs of mint—and, perhaps, a festive paper parasol—and serve.

FOOD FOR THOUGHT

- Daddy longlegs aren't spiders. They belong to an entirely different order, the Opiliones (also known as harvestmen) and are more closely related to ticks and mites than they are to spiders.
- *Meganeura*, a now-extinct dragonfly from the Carboniferous period (250 million years ago), had a wingspan of over two feet.
- When captured, giant water bugs may "play possum," feigning death for as long as fifteen minutes.
- The erratic steps of the tarantella, an Italian folk dance, mimic the frenzied movements of a spider-bite victim.
- Lacking organs of insertion, male centipedes must deposit their sperm packets and pray that female centipedes will decide to pick them up.

SWEET AND SOUR SILKWORM

Yield: 4 servings

Factory workers often eat silkworms (*Bombyx mori*) as soon as the insects have finished weaving their valuable cocoons. The first step in processing the silk involves dropping the cocoons into hot water, cooking the live silkworm pupae within. Surplus silkworm pupae are eaten throughout the Guangdong province of southeastern China, one of Asia's largest silk producers. In Japan, the same by-products of the silk trade are fried, canned, and sold at supermarkets—the food of the future for 150 yen.

If you live anywhere but the silk-growing districts, start planning your all-you-can-eat silkworm feeds well in advance. You'll have to grow your own, from eggs the size of a grain of sand, no less, which can take anywhere from a month to a month and a half. Rearing silkworms is like caring for a newborn child: fresh from the egg, the larvae can barely take care of themselves. The only thing they'll eat are mulberry leaves, and these must be replaced at least once a day. It's been estimated that the silkworms from one ounce of eggs will gorge themselves on approximately 1,500 pounds of leaves.

All this food and round-the-clock attention is not wasted on the silkworm larva, which increases its size ten-thousand-fold over the days between hatching and pupation. It outgrows its skin several times, molting until it reaches its peak size, about two and a half inches. Then it starts spinning a cocoon. Left to its own devices, the worm would undergo a final metamorphosis, eventually breaking open its silken wrapper to emerge as an adult *Bombyx* moth. Follow my recipe for Silkworm Stir-Fry and you'll probably never see this grand finale.

---

1 teaspoon cornstarch

$^1/_4$ cup water

2 tablespoons vegetable oil

1 teaspoon finely chopped garlic

1 yellow onion, halved and thinly sliced

1 tomato, quartered

8 to 10 canned pineapple chunks (about 2 ounces)

1 carrot, cut into thin rounds

2 tablespoons light soy sauce

1 teaspoon sugar

Freshly ground pepper to taste

12 frozen silkworm pupae, thawed

1. In a small bowl, stir together the cornstarch and water. Set aside.

2. In a wok, heat the oil over medium-high heat. Add the garlic and fry until golden.

3. Add all the remaining ingredients one at a time, saving the silkworm pupae until last, and cook, stirring constantly, for 3 or 4 minutes.

4. When vegetables are still slightly crispy, add the cornstarch mixture and stir briefly to thicken and coat the ingredients.

5. Transfer to a plate and serve immediately.

AMPLE DRUMSTICKS

Yield: 4 servings

Meaning "one hundred legger" in Latin, the name "centipede" is a slight exaggeration. Few of these arthropods are graced with more than thirty pairs of limbs, and the common house centipede, *Scutigera coleoptrata*, sports a mere fifteen. Still, if you live in a household where everyone lusts for the turkey's two drumsticks, then this edible arthropod—a member of the invertebrate class Chilopoda—was created for you.

Realize, however, that there's not much meat on one centipede limb. Each jointed foot contains just a few strands of tissue—the paired tendons that jerk the feet rapidly forward and back, helping the living centipede reach its top racing speeds. So if you're planning to serve centipedes at your next sit-down affair, leave the limbs attached to their corresponding body segments. In this way, a judicious carver can divide a single centipede among twelve to forty-eight diners, depending on the species he or she has opted to prepare.

Of course, you can also offer each guest their own centipede, as the following recipe suggests. My favorite choice for this recipe, the so-called giant redheaded centipede, or *Scolopendra heros*, is a handsome ocher and honey-colored invertebrate with twenty-two body segments and forty-four legs, and it can reach a length of six to eight inches. Prized by members of Venezuela's Guahibo tribe, the giant centipede, *S. gigantea*, is a full four to six inches larger—the perfect substitute for Cornish game hen!

The slightly fishy flavor of centipede flesh is neatly balanced by the sweet-and-sour taste of seasoned soy sauce, thinly applied as a glaze. My favorite formula for such flavoring comes from Braiden Rex-Johnson, author of several books on Northwest seafood. I've slightly modified her recipe here for my purposes.

WARNING: AVOID THIS DEADLY ALTERNATIVE

Millipedes (class Diplopoda) should *never* be substituted for centipedes in a dish. These animals secrete a foul-smelling fluid that, in some species, may contain traces of hydrogen cyanide—not good, unless you're from the Borgia household.

1 tablespoon vegetable oil

1 tablespoon soy sauce

1 tablespoon brown sugar

1 tablespoon garlic powder

2 tablespoons freshly grated ginger

4 frozen giant Sonoran centipedes, thawed

1. Preheat the broiler and lightly oil the rack of a broiling pan.

2. In a small bowl, mix together the oil, soy sauce, brown sugar, and garlic powder. Add the grated ginger and blend thoroughly.

3. Set centipedes on the prepared broiling pan. Brush the centipedes with about half of the glaze, then broil them 3 to 4 inches from the heat source for 3 minutes. Remove from heat, turn centipedes, and brush them with the remaining glaze. Broil for another 3 minutes, then serve warm.

NOTE: Before cooking and serving any centipede, snip off the toxignaths, or "poison jaws," on the animal's head. These paired appendages can be deterrents to any plucky person who nibbles on this part of the centipede's anatomy. The name Chilopoda, by the way, is Latin for "lip-foot," a reference to the fact that these "jaws" are really modified legs. Isn't nature wonderful? A centipede's genital openings are located on the second to the last body segment. If you think anyone will be hip to this anatomical oddity, you may want to remove this part as well.

SPIN-AKOPITA

Yield: 4 servings

" There was an old lady who swallowed a spider. I don't know why she swallowed the spider. I'm glad she tried 'er. " —DGG

"If in the past we have been hoodwinked by lurid mariners' tales of man-eating spiders, we are now on our guard and sometimes find it difficult to believe that there really are spider-eating men," wrote William Bristowe, Britain's eminent authority on the eight-legged set. His paper *Spider Superstitions and Folklore* contains a convincing roster of arachnophagous folk, from an unidentified strumpet in the court of Alexander the Great to one of Bristowe's contemporaries, novelist Sax Rohmer, who claimed to have cured himself of a fear of spiders by eating one.

As further proof that people will sup on spiders, Bristowe recounted his own experiences in northern Thailand, where two kinds of spider, the giant orb-weaving *Nephila maculata* and the hairy blue *Melopoeus albostriatus*, are favorites of the Lao hill tribe. The flavor of this second species, when toasted, was like "the marrow of chicken bones or perhaps Brand's chicken essence," according to the Englishman.

Bristowe noted that the protein and fat content of toasted spiders (established as 63.4 percent and 9.8 percent, respectively) may be important dietary supplements, offsetting the Lao's overdependence on rice. But even among cultures whose diets are more nutritious and varied, spiders are regarded as fair game. Native North Americans, South African Bushmen, aborigines of Australia, indigenous people of Gambia and Senegal, and the original inhabitants of the West Indies, New Caledonia, and Madagascar all ate spiders, raw and cooked, whenever they had the chance.

In his seventeenth-century treatise, Thomas Mouffet suggested an array of medicinal uses for spiders and their webs in particular, which were routinely applied as bandages to wounds. The cure for jaundice in Mouffet's day entailed rolling a live spider in butter and swallowing it as a pill. House spider excrement was also held in high esteem. Mixed with rose oil and saffron, it was the favored treatment for eye infections. As Mouffet put it, "there is nothing so filthy in a spider that is not good for something."

The most celebrated spider eater, by the way, was Mouffet's daughter, Patience. I have it on good authority that she frequently became a human guinea pig for her father's experiments with entomophagy, a role for which she was later immortalized in the nursery rhyme "Little Miss Muffet."

In my recipe for Spin-akopita, a dish of Greek origin, the main ingredient is the common Northwest wolf spider, *Pardosa vancouveri*, a seasonally ubiquitous being with fuzzy black legs and a fat body about $3/8$ inch long. I've filled a quart Mason jar with these sun-loving souls, which I caught in my sweep net while they were trying to bask in the warm rays of early summer. There are over a hundred species in this genus, the members of which are scattered throughout North America and much of Europe. No special preparation is needed for incorporating these animals in any number of stir-fries and stews. If you can successfully manipulate sheets of filo dough, you should have no problem handling this recipe's spider-intensive filling.

2 tablespoons olive oil

1 small yellow onion, chopped

1 clove garlic, minced

3 eggs

$^1/_4$ pound feta cheese

1 package (12-ounces) frozen spinach, defrosted and drained

$^1/_4$ cup chopped fresh parsley

$^1/_2$ teaspoon oregano

Freshly ground black pepper to taste

24 medium-sized wolf spiders

4 tablespoons ($^1/_2$ stick) butter

$^1/_2$ pound of phyllo dough

1. In a sauté pan, heat the olive oil, then sauté the onions and garlic until they are light brown.

2. Beat the eggs in a large bowl, crumbling in the feta cheese. Add spinach, parsley, oregano, pepper, and spiders, then stir in the onion and garlic.

3. Melt the butter. Use some of it to brush the bottom of an 8 by 8-inch baking pan. The rest will be for buttering the phyllo dough.

4. Preheat the oven to 375°F.

5. Lay six sheets of the phyllo dough, one sheet at a time, on the bottom of the baking pan. The ends of each sheet should extend over the edges of the pan. Brush the top of every other sheet with butter.

6. Spread spider-and-spinach mixture evenly over the layer of phyllo dough. Fold in the edges of the phyllo dough, partially covering this layer.

7. With the remaining phyllo sheets, make another layer on top, again buttering the tops of every second sheet. Trim the overhanging edges and make $^1/_2$-inch-deep slashes in the top with a sharp knife.

8. Bake uncovered until the dough turns a golden brown, about 35 to 40 minutes. Allow to cool slightly, then cut into four 2-inch squares.

SKY PRAWN

Yield: 6 servings

Dragonflies—or "winged bullets," to quote Edwin Way Teale—are the original fast food. They can fly at speeds of thirty-five miles an hour, reverse direction in midair, and, if the situation requires it, suddenly slam on the brakes, taking a perch on a slender poolside reed without missing a wingbeat.

Bug catchers know that nabbing a dragonfly is like shagging a tennis ball during a tourney at Wimbeldon. Stand for hours at the edge of a pond, waving a butterfly net and praying, and sooner or later your efforts will probably pay off.

Or you can try the method perfected by the Balinese. To capture live dragonflies, these enterprising Indonesian islanders are said to take a stiff piece of wire and attach a gob of latex-like sap from a jackfruit tree to its tip. They then fasten the wire to a short length of bamboo or wood. The finished product (called a *ngoneng*) is then carried to the water's edge and whirled briskly, which causes the wire's sticky tip to spin. Apparently the circular movement entices the predatory dragonflies to pounce, and they invariably gum themselves up in the jackfruit goo.

Regardless of how you gather your dragonflies, you should consider cooking them in the traditional, time-honored way. The following recipe is freely adapted from Robert W. Pemberton's article "Catching and Eating Dragonflies in Bali and Elsewhere in Asia," which appeared in an issue of the journal *American Entomologist*. The name for this dish, Sky Prawn, was supplied by a friend who ordered this very entrée at a restaurant in the village of Ubud, on the island of Bali.

---

20 frozen green darners or other large-bodied dragonfly species, thawed

2 tablespoons vegetable oil

1 clove garlic, finely chopped

2 shallots, finely chopped

1 tablespoon freshly grated ginger

1 cup coconut milk

$^1/_3$ cup sliced bamboo shoots

3 whole baby sweet corn, sliced lengthwise into strips

1 carrot, cut into thin rounds

1 tablespoon light soy sauce

1 teaspoon sugar

2 large fresh red chiles, cut into thin strips

6 sprigs of cilantro

Cooked brown or white long-grain rice for serving

1. Wash the green darners and pat dry. Remove their wings and set aside to use as garnish.

2. In a cast-iron wok, heat the oil over high heat. Add the garlic, shallots, and ginger and sauté for no more than 1 minute. Stir in the coconut milk.

3. Add the green darners, bamboo shoots, corn, carrot, soy sauce, sugar, and chiles and stir well. Lower the heat to medium and continue cooking, stirring until the vegetable are al dente. Transfer the mixture to a serving bowl.

4. Garnish with the cilantro sprigs and green darner wings and serve on a bed of rice.

HARVESTING HINT

My Seattle friend Don Ehlen, an experienced collector of all things small and spineless, told me of a good way to grab dragonflies, offering me eight freshly caught green darners, *Anax junius*, as proof of his prowess. Don's secret? Wait until dark and, using a flashlight, check the underside of leaves on trees fringing the dragonflies' favorite waterways. In deep states of slumber, the world-champion stunt fliers are sitting ducks for skilled handpickers like Don.

Travels with My Ant: Scorpion Husbandry on the Road

In the 1990s, when the mood at airports was considerably more relaxed, I would occasionally travel with live scorpions in small cottage cheese containers, which were stapled shut and nestled amid the T-shirts and socks in my checked bags. In this way I could keep my essential ingredients alive and well while I traveled.

Heightened airport security, in particular mandatory inspections of baggage, put an end to that. Think about it. If the security personnel are confiscating passengers' nail clippers, imagine what would happen if they happened upon venomous arthropods in my suitcase.

When I'd arrive at my hotel, I'd unpack my bags, remove the scorpions, and set them aside. But that wasn't the end of it. Most hotel rooms, especially in the South, are kept quite cool year-round. Because scorpions are desert dwellers, accustomed to heat and aridity, they don't share my appreciation for air-conditioning. To keep my mini-livestock happy during their final days on this planet, I'd balance their cartons on top of the room's TV set. Then I'd press the "on" button and shut the doors to the entertainment center, thus capturing the warmth from the TV's big cathode ray tube.

Of course I'd have to leave myself a note, reminding myself to relocate the containers in the morning, lest a hapless maid should discover my thermophilic travel companions. The best place to hide the scorpions? That turned out to be the drawer in my bedside table—the one with a Gideon Bible in it. Hardly anyone looks in there.

ODONATE HORS D'OEUVRES

Yield: 6 servings

The first bug that Zack Lemann ate was a live fire ant, after making a bet with a school chum when he was seven years old. "Not one of my shining moments," he later admitted.

As a grown-up, Zack has earned his reputation as a top-notch bug chef, sharing his knowledge of entomophagy with appreciative throngs. On a busy week as many as ten thousand people sample Zack's Cajun-spiced crickets and mealworm snacks.

More to the point, however, Zack can boast one thing that no other chef can: he's beaten me, the Bug Chef, in cooking competitions on three separate occasions. And were it not for Hurricane Charley, he probably would've defeated me again at the North Carolina Museum of Natural Sciences' annual BugFest, back in 2004. So let me present one of the recipes Zack used against me to win the judges' favor at all three events. It's guaranteed to win your high approval.

SAUCE
2 tablespoons butter
2 tablespoons light soy sauce
2 tablespoons Dijon mustard
Pinch of garlic powder

1 large egg
4 ounces Zatarain's Seasoned Fish Fry or other seafood breading mix
1 tablespoon butter
$^1/_2$ cup canola oil
2 medium portobello mushrooms, cut into slices $^1/_4$ inch thick
12 frozen green darner dragonflies, thawed

1. To make the sauce, in a small skillet over low heat, melt the butter. Add the remaining sauce ingredients and stir to combine. Transfer to a small ramekin and set aside.

2. In a small bowl, beat the egg. Pour the breading mix into a separate bowl.

3. Set two small skillets on the stovetop, each over medium to medium-high heat. Add the butter to one skillet and the oil to the other.

4. When the butter has melted, add the mushroom slices to that pan. Cook until browned, approximately 2 minutes. Transfer the mushrooms to paper towels to drain.

5. While the mushrooms are cooking, use tweezers to hold one dragonfly at a time by its wings, gently coating both sides of the insect with egg, and then dredging the insect in the breading mix.

6. Add individual dragonflies to the hot oil, making sure they don't stick to each other as you add them. Sauté until the exoskeletons of the dragonflies darken—30 seconds to 1 minute per side, depending on the size of the insect and the temperature of the oil.

7. Arrange the mushroom slices on a serving platter and place a dragonfly atop each mushroom slice. Add a small dollop of sauce to each hors d'oeurve before serving.

SCORPION SCALOPPINE

Yield: 4 servings

Scorpions look plenty like crabs or crayfish, so it's logical that they'd be just as tasty. But because these well-armed invertebrates can pack quite a venomous punch, I've always thought that only the most daring of chefs would try to make meals out of them.

Not so, says Ronald Taylor. In Morocco and Egypt there exists a long-standing guild of scorpion eaters. "The profession belongs to families," Taylor writes, "and by heredity the members of these families are said to be immune to scorpion stings."

Professional scorpion eaters are often called in to cleanse a house that has been left vacant for some time. "The scorpion-eater will squat on the floor in the middle of the room and begin to whistle softly," explains Taylor. "The scorpions appear from their hiding places and walk across the floor toward him. . . . The scorpion-eater picks up the scorpions and puts them in a bag. When he is finished, he takes the scorpions home and he and his family eat them."

If you think whistling for scorpions sounds absurd, check out how many collectors in Texas and Arizona fill their goody bags. After dark, these brave hearts take to the highways, where desert scorpions congregate, apparently to absorb the heat stored in the sun-baked blacktop. The collectors scan the road shoulders, using handheld black lights to illuminate the objects of their quest. They know that a scorpion's exoskeleton will glow in the dark, making it stand out like an old Fillmore poster against the subdued nocturnal sandscape.

I launched my scorpion-eating era with a phone call to Barney Tomberlin of Portal, Arizona. Barney supplies live insects to insect zoos and nature centers throughout the United States and, perhaps because of his proximity to the Sonoran Desert, on occasion rustles up the odd rattlesnake for a TV shoot. He sold me my initial six desert hairy scorpions (*Hadrurus arizonensis*), formidable four- to seven-inch animals with honey- and charcoal-colored bodies and four o'clock shadows of sensory hairs on their limbs. In the quantities I now acquire from Barney—twenty-five or thirty "Live Harmless Invertebrates," as their shipping boxes clearly state—I get a deal: $12.50 each, plus shipping. That's not a bad price to pay for the largest scorpion in North America.

Sometimes, however, I'll use emperor scorpions (*Pandinus imperator*) instead. These natives of Africa are even bigger-bodied than Desert Hairys, and their claws are *humongous*. But there's something about their shiny black body armor that's not very visually appealing. And that confirms my belief that sight plays a large part in our selection and acceptance of new foods.

continued

2 cups low-fat milk

8 frozen desert hairy scorpions or a similar
   species, thawed

1 cup white cornmeal

2 tablespoons butter

1 tablespoon fresh lemon juice

2 tablespoons chopped fresh parsley

1. Pour the milk into a medium bowl. Add
    the scorpions to the bowl and set aside
    while preparing the rest of the ingredients.
    Spread the cornmeal on a plate and set
    aside.

2. In a large skillet, melt the butter over high
    heat. Working with one scorpion at a time,
    remove them from the milk, allowing the
    excess to drain off. Dredge the scorpions
    through the cornmeal, shaking off any
    excess.

3. Place the scorpions in the hot butter and
    cook until they are golden brown, about
    2 minutes. Then turn the scorpions over
    and cook until done, about 1 minute more.

4. Drain on paper towels. Sprinkle with lemon
    juice and chopped parsley and serve.

WARNING: HANDLE WITH CARE

I had always suspected that the pain of a scorpion's sting was greatly exaggerated and that, like a tarantula's bite, it was no worse than that of a bee. Then I met Jane Stevens, curator of the Monsanto Insectarium at the St. Louis Zoo, and she set me straight.

Years ago Jane was stung on the finger by an exceptionally large scorpion—probably a nonnative species that had somehow escaped into the wilds of Missouri. She explained that the pain was intense, "the kind where you hear someone screaming, and then you realize that someone is you." Her friends rushed Jane to the nearest hospital, a forty-five-minute drive from the scene of the sting. In the emergency room she was given antihistamines, some Motrin, and a shot of Demerol. When these failed to dull the pain, the physicians on duty administered an even stronger topical anesthetic.

"I started feeling like Elvis in Las Vegas," Jane recalls, "but my hand still throbbed with electricity." The severe pain in her hand continued for two days, and her finger remained sensitive for another eight weeks.

So here's my advice, and that of Jane, too: handle any live scorpion, regardless of its size, with the utmost care. After it is frozen solid, each scorpion should have its terminal tail segment—the one that contains the paired venom glands and the hollow, curved barb—removed with a sharp knife. In parts of China, where platefuls of scorpions are standard restaurant fare, the scorpions are cooked and served with the stinger and venom gland still attached. However, the Chinese use much smaller scorpions in their cooking, and the act of cooking may denature the venom at any rate.

PARTY PUPAE

Yield: 6 servings of 2 pupae each

Native North Americans knew a good moth when they saw one. In California, they went after the caterpillars of the white-lined sphinx moth (*Hyles leneata*), a fat and juicy species similar to the green tomato hornworm, with great zeal.

Other California tribes sought the pupae of the pandora moth (*Coloradia pandora*), a major defoliator of pine trees in the West. The pupae of these insects and the closely related saturniid moths were amassed by the hundreds, dried, and stowed away for wintertime use.

Saturniid moth cocoons look like packets of leaves ingeniously sewn together by fairies. But like the silkworm's cocoons, they're made of silk, spun by the caterpillar, the shed skin of which can usually be found scrunched down at one end of the cocoon. Saturniids manufacture these designer packages in the autumn months. Inside each package lies a moth-in-waiting, a dark brown chitinous sphere, its inside filled with liquid nutrients—the raw materials for the adult moth, which will be built in the spring.

From a chef's perspective, saturniids come prepackaged in their own parchment paper, that is, they can be baked "as is" in an oven preheated to 375°F. Remove them from the heat after about 20 minutes, slit the silk outer wrap and, after waiting a few minutes for the pupae to cool, pop this nutty, liquid-filled bit into your mouth. Now go ahead and chew—I dare you. If you've the courage for it, my Party Pupae recipe is only slightly more complicated than this.

ENTO-EPHEMERA

Perhaps providing us with too much information, ethnographer William Greenwood Wright described the harvest of three- and four-inch-long sphinx moth caterpillars by California's Cahuilla tribe at the close of the nineteenth century. "Seizing a fat worm, they pull off its head, and by a dexterous jerk, the viscera are ejected and the wriggling carcass is put into a small basket or bag," he wrote. Wright also told of the great worm feasts, at which the sphinx moth caterpillars were featured—"a time of great rejoicing" that attracted guests from many miles around.

1 cup all-purpose flour
$^1/_2$ teaspoon baking powder
$^1/_4$ teaspoon salt
$1^1/_2$ teaspoons vegetable shortening
$^1/_3$ cup milk
12 saturniid moth pupae, baked (as described above)
Melted butter for brushing

1. In a mixing bowl, combine the flour, baking powder, and salt. Using your fingers, cut in the shortening until the mixture resembles coarse crumbs. Gradually add the milk and stir to form a soft dough.

2. On a lightly floured board, knead the dough for 2 to 3 minutes. Roll out dough to form a 12 by 6-inch rectangle, approximately $1/4$ to $1/2$-inch thick. Cut the rectangle into twelve 2 by 3-inch strips.

3. Wrap one strip around each moth pupa, letting one end of the pupa peek out.

4. Place the dough-wrapped pupae in a greased pan and brush each with melted butter. Cover and let rest for 20 minutes. Meanwhile, preheat the oven to 425°F.

5. Bake until nicely browned, about 15 minutes. Remove from the oven, transfer to a serving platter, and serve warm.

HARVESTING HINT

You can buy saturniid cocoons (each filled with a live pupae) from Carolina Biological Supply and a few other retail sources. These animals are not taken from the wild but have been bred in captivity, so I've no guilt about incorporating them into my meal plans. I prefer their Moth Cocoon set—three each of the larger saturniid species, one of which is likely to be the breathtakingly elegant luna moth (*Actins luna*).

DEEP-FRIED TARANTULA SPIDER

Yield: 4 servings

Readers of earlier printings of my cookbook were treated to the sad tale of my failed attempt to acquire specimens of the world's biggest arachnid, the goliath bird-eating spider (*Theraphosa blondi*) as the pièce de résistance of this recipe collection. Since then, I've had many opportunities to cook with lesser-sized tarantulas and have now replaced the original "hypothetical" recipe with the one on these pages. Although I am at times saddened to dispatch such charismatic and long-lived invertebrates in the name of bug cuisine, I console myself with the thought that most of the tarantulas I've acquired were otherwise destined to unsatisfying lives as classroom pets and lab research specimens.

Furthermore, let's face it: tarantulas make for a tasty and texturally satisfying meal. Here's why. Unlike heavily armored grasshoppers, beetles, and other land arthropods, tarantulas wear an outer layer of chitin that is comparatively thin and pliable. That's right: their eight muscular limbs are chewy, not crunchy. As such, the plentiful meat on one of these animals is more accessible and, hence, the makings for a savory spider soirée.

If, for my birthday dinner, I could order anything I wanted, I'd request a Maine lobster or a tarantula spider. Properly prepared, either would make an awesome celebratory entrée.

Incidentally, this particlular recipe helped me best three other chefs in a series of round-robin eliminations, assisting me in bringing home the gold at the first-ever Big Bug Cook-Off, held in May 2011 at the Natural History Museum of Los Angeles County.

2 cups canola or vegetable oil

2 frozen adult Texas brown, Chilean rose, or similar-sized tarantulas, thawed

1 cup tempura batter (page 84)

1 teaspoon smoked paprika

1. In a deep saucepan or deep-fat fryer, heat the oil to 350°F.

2. With a sharp knife, sever and discard the abdomens from the two tarantulas. Singe off any of the spider's body hairs with a crème brûlée torch or butane cigarette lighter.

3. Dip each spider into the tempura batter to thoroughly coat. Use a slotted spoon or your hands to make sure each spider is spread-eagled (so to speak) and not clumped together before dropping it into the hot oil.

4. Deep-fry the spiders, one at a time, until the batter is lightly browned, about 1 minute. Remove each spider from the oil and place it on paper towels to drain.

5. Use a sharp knife to cut each spider in two lengthwise. Sprinkle with the paprika and serve. Encourage your guests to try the legs first and, if still hungry, to nibble on the meat-filled mesothorax, avoiding the spider's paired fangs, which are tucked away in the head region.

RESOURCES

For More Information

Bodenheimer, F. S. *Insects as Human Food.* The Hague: Dr. W. Junk Publishers, 1951.

Durst, Patrick B., Dennis V. Johnson, Robin N. Leslie, and Kenichi Shono, eds. *Forest Insects: Humans Bite Back.* Bangkok: Food and Agriculture Organization of the United Nations, Regional Office for Asia and the Pacific, 2010.

Holt, Vincent M. *Why Not Eat Insects?* London: Field & Tuer, the Leadenhall Press, E.C., 1885.

Menzel, Peter, and Faith D'Aluisio, *Man Eating Bugs: The Art and Science of Eating Insects.* Berkeley, CA: Ten Speed Press, 1998.

Ramos-Elorduy, Julieta. *Creepy Crawly Cuisine: The Gourmet Guide to Edible Insects.* South Paris, ME: Park Street Press, 1998.

Taylor, Ronald L. *Butterflies in My Stomach.* Santa Barbara, CA: Woodbridge Press, 1975.

Taylor, Ronald L., and Barbara J. Carter. *Entertaining with Insects.* Santa Barbara, CA: Woodbridge Press, 1976.

Suppliers of Edible Arthropods

Carolina Biological Supply Company
2700 York Road
Burlington, NC 27215
www.carolina.com
800-334-5551
Ants, bees, moth cocoons, centipedes, cockroaches, crickets, mealworms, scorpions, superworms, spiders, tarantulas, termites, and wax worms

Connecticut Valley Biological
P.O. Box 326
Southampton, MA 01073
www.connecticutvalleybiological.com
800-628-7748
Ants, butterfly and moth cocoons, cockroaches, crickets, mealworms, superworms, and wax worms

Fluker Farms
P.O. Box 530
Port Allen, LA 70767-4087
www.flukerfarms.com
800-735-8537
Crickets, mealworms, and superworms

Grubco
7995 North Gilomore Road
Fairfield, OH 45014
www.grubco.com
800-222-3563
*Crickets, mealworms, superworms, and
wax worms*

Hatari Invertebrates
P.O. Box 16510
Portal, AZ 85632
www.bugsofamerica.com
520-558-2418
*Centipedes, katydids, lubber grasshoppers,
scorpions, and spiders*

Linda's Gone Buggie
P.O. Box 5047
Lake Station, IN 46405
www.lindasgonebuggie.com
219-299-0174
*Silkworms, hornworms, mealworms, and
superworms*

Reeves Cricket Ranch
3207 Hughes Road
Everson, WA 98247
360-966-3300
*Crickets, mealworms, superworms, and
wax worms*

SmallStock Food Strategies
53 Savoy Street
Providence, RI 02906
www.smallstockfoods.com
401-286-9065
*Cambodian crickets, giant water bugs, leafcutter
ants, Thai locusts, and other exotic food insects*

Timberline Live Pet Foods
201 East Timberline Road
Marion, IL 62959
www.timberlinefisheries.com
800-423-2248
*Crickets, mealworms, superworms, and
wax worms*

Sellers of Prepared Edible Arthropods

Chapul
222 S. Main Street
Suite 500
Salt Lake City, UT 84101
www.chapul.com
801-896-4515
*Chaco Bars and Thai Bars, both made from
crickets*

Fluker Farms
P.O. Box 530
Port Allen, LA 70767-4087
www.flukerfarms.com
800-735-8537
Chocolate-covered crickets

Hot Lix
P.O. Box 447
Grover Beach, CA 93483
www.hotlix.com
800-328-9676
*Assorted insect snacks, including Larvets,
Cricket Lick-It suckers, and Amber
InsectNside candy*

Suppliers of Arthropod Care and Collecting Gear

BioQuip Products
2321 Gladwick Street
Rancho Dominguez, CA 90220
www.bioquip.com
310-667-8800

Carolina Biological Supply Company
2700 York Road
Burlington, NC 27215
www.carolina.com
800-334-5551

Connecticut Valley Biological
P.O. Box 326
Southampton, MA 01073
www.connecticutvalleybiological.com
800-628-7748

Ward's Natural Science
P.O. Box 92912
Rochester, NY 14623
http://wardsci.com
800-962-2660

Sponsors of Bug-Eating Events

Audubon Butterfly Garden and Insectarium
423 Canal Street
U.S. Custom House
New Orleans, LA 70130
www.auduboninstitute.org
504-581-4629
The Bug Appétit café offers daily bug-cooking demonstrations and samples.

Cafe Racer
5828 Roosevelt Way NE
Seattle, WA 98105
http://caferacerseattle.com/
206-523-5282
The Feast of Saint Gratus Bug Banquet is held each year on November 7.

Garfield Park Nature Center
11350 Broadway Avenue
Garfield Heights, OH 44125
216-341-3152
The Annual Bug Fest features chef Gene White, plus mealworm races and games for kids in early August.

Missouri Department of Conservation
701 James McCarthy Drive
St. Joseph, MO 64507
http://mdc.mo.gov/regions/northwest
816-271-3100
Held on the second Saturday of September, Insect-O-Rama offers cockroach races and the culinary creations of insect chef Paul Landkamer.

Natural History Museum of Los Angeles County
900 Exposition Boulevard
Los Angeles, CA 90007
www.nhm.org/site/activities-programs/bug-fair
213-763-3388
The largest two-day insect event in the United States, the museum's annual Bug Fair includes bug-cooking demonstrations and plenty of free samples on a weekend in mid-May.

North Carolina Museum of Natural Sciences
121 West Jones Street
Raleigh, NC 27601
http://naturalsciences.org/
919-707-9800
BugFest, the largest one-day insect event, held in late summer or early fall, features the famous Cafe Insecta, with an assortment of arthropod snacks.

Pennsylvania State University
Department of Entomology
501 ASI Building
University Park, PA 16802
http://ento.psu.edu
814-865-1895
The yearly Great Insect Fair in September features the Insect Deli and a honey-tasting lab.

Purdue University
Department of Entomology
901 West State Street
West Lafayette, IN 47907
https://ag.purdue.edu/entm/Pages/default.aspx
765-494-2089
The Bug Café and Big Bug Bake-Off are offered in conjunction with Purdue's annual Bug Bowl event in April.

State Botanical Garden of Georgia
South Milledge Avenue
Athens, Georgia 30602
http://botgarden.uga.edu
706-542-1244
The annual September Insectival features a smorgasbord of edible insects.

The University of Texas at Austin
Austin, Texas 78703
512-232-5833
Two public events have entomophagy themes: an annual Fright at the Museum on a day near Halloween and the semiannual Insecta Fiesta in April.

Helpful Websites

Food Insects Newsletter
www.foodinsectsnewsletter.org

Girl Meets Bug
http://girlmeetsbug.com

World Entomophagy
http://WorldEnto.com

INDEX

A

Allergies, 16–17, 55
Alpha-Bait Soup, 91
Amaretto Honeypots, 65–66
Ample Drumsticks, 106–7
Ant Jemima's Buckwheat-Bug
    Griddlecakes, 63
Ants
    Amaretto Honeypots, 65–66
    Ant Jemima's Buckwheat-Bug
        Griddlecakes, 63
    Ants in Pants, 67
    formic acid and, 62
    harvesting, 61–62
    nutritional value of, 4
    Pear Salad with Chiangbai
        Ants, 69
    seasonal availability of, 12
    species of, 63, 65, 69
Asparagus
    Cream of Katydid Soup, 35

B

Basil
    Pest-o, 90
Batesian mimicry, 16
Beans
    Alpha-Bait Soup, 91
    Really Hoppin' John, 43
Bees
    Bee's Knees, 60
    buying, 55–56
    cooking tips for, 57
    Glory Bee, 57
    nutritional value of, 54
    stings from, 16, 55

threats to, 56, 91
    Three Bee Salad, 59
Beverages, 17
Bible, bugs in the, 21, 33, 39, 48
Blister beetles, 98–99
Bodenheimer, F. S., 50, 54, 96
Bread, St. John's, 38–39
Bristowe, William, 108
Buchmann, Stephen, 12
Buckwheat-Bug Griddlecakes, Ant
    Jemima's, 63
Bugs
    allergies to, 16–17, 55
    anatomy of, 14–15
    buying, 11, 12, 21, 72, 120–21
    characteristics of edible, 97
    cooking techniques for, 13–14
    definition of, 1–2
    facts about, 2, 20, 48, 74, 104
    food regulations for, 9–10, 16
    harvesting, 11–12, 72–73, 122
    for healing, 98–99
    inedible, 16–17
    measuring, 13
    nutritional value of, 4
    raising, 15–16
    raw, 11
    seasonal availability of, 12
    species diversity of, 96
    See also Entomophagy (bug
        eating); individual bugs
Bugs in a Rug, 31

C

Carob
    St. John's Bread, 38–39

Carson, Johnny, 31
Carter, Barbara, 31, 60, 93
Centipedes
    Ample Drumsticks, 106–7
    anatomy of, 106
    species of, 106
Cereals
    Chirpy Chex Party Mix, 28–29
    Termite Treats, 53
Chapulines con Chocolate Fondue, 45
Cheese
    Pear Salad with Chiangbai Ants, 69
    Pest-o, 90
    Piz-zz-zz-za, 88–89
    Spin-akopita, 108–9
Chex Party Mix, Chirpy, 28–29
Children, as bug eaters, 37, 66
Chirpy Chex Party Mix, 28–29
Chitin, 6, 14
Chocolate
    Ants in Pants, 67
    Chapulines con Chocolate
        Fondue, 45
    Chocolate Cricket Torte, 32
Cicadas
    harvesting, 88
    life cycle of, 88
    Piz-zz-zz-za, 88–89
Cockchafers, 73
Cockroaches
    buying, 78
    Cockroach à la King, 78–79
    cooking tips for, 78
    seasonal availability of, 12
    species of, 78

Coconut
    Bee's Knees, 60
    Sky Prawn, 110–11
Collman, Sharon, 90
Cookies, White Chocolate and Wax
    Worm, 93
Cooking techniques, 13–14
Corn
    Niblets and Cricklets, 25
    Sky Prawn, 110–11
Cream of Katydid Soup, 35
Crickets
    Bugs in a Rug, 31
    buying, 23–24
    Chirpy Chex Party Mix, 28–29
    Chocolate Cricket Torte, 32
    cooking tips for, 24
    Cricket Seasoning à la Vij's, 30
    Crispy Crickets, 29
    harvesting, 22, 23
    measuring, 13
    Niblets and Cricklets, 25
    noise from, 24
    nutritional value of, 4, 24
    Orthopteran Orzo, 27
    Piz-zz-zz-za, 88–89
    raising, 16
    Really Hoppin' John, 43
    seasonal availability of, 12
    storing, 24
Crispy Crickets, 29
Curried Termite Stew, 52

D
Deep-Fried Tarantula Spider, 119
DeFoliart, Gene, 8
Dhalwala, Meeru, 10, 30
Dragonflies
    harvesting, 110, 111
    Odonate Hors d'Oeuvres, 112
    Sky Prawn, 110–11
Dunkel, Florence, 8, 9

E
Ehlen, Don, 111
Elorduy, Julieta Ramos, 98
Entomophagy (bug eating)
    benefits of, 4–7
    changing attitudes toward, 9
    by children, 37, 66
    events for, 9, 32, 69, 79, 112, 119,
        122–23

facts about, 16
health inspectors and, 82
history of, 2–3, 21–22
nutrition and, 4
prevalence of, 2
by primates, 41
proponents of, 7–9, 10–11, 38, 83
regional attitudes toward, 79
resources for, 7–9, 120–23
Euro, Joe, 17

F
Fluker Farms, 21
Fondue, Chocolate, Chapulines
    con, 45
Food and Drug Administration
    (FDA), 9–10, 16
Formic acid, 62
Fossey, Dian, 41

G
Giant water bugs
    Giant Water Bug on Watercress,
        100–101
    harvesting, 100–101
    nutritional value of, 4
    seasonal availability of, 12
    Watermelon and Water Bug
        Surprise, 103–4
Glory Bee, 57
Gracer, Dave, 10, 103
Grasshoppers
    Chapulines con Chocolate
        Fondue, 45
    harvesting, 34
    nutritional value of, 4
    Oaxacan Whoppers, 36
    raising, 16
    Really Hoppin' John, 43
    seasonal availability of, 12
    Sheeshi Kabobs, 41–42
    species of, 36, 45
Gratus, Saint, 69

H
Healing, bugs for, 98–99
Holt, Vincent M., 7, 72–73, 78
Hoppin' John, Really, 43
Hymenoptera, 48. See also Ants;
    Bees; Wasps

J
John the Baptist, 38

K
Kabobs, Sheeshi, 41–42
Katydids
    Cream of Katydid Soup, 35
    harvesting, 34
    identifying, 33
    seasonal availability of, 12
    Sheeshi Kabobs, 41–42
Katzen, Mollie, 52

L
Latkes, Larval (a.k.a. Grubsteaks),
    80
Lemann, Zack, 10, 28, 112
Lewis, Branden, 103
Lloyd, Monte, 88
Locusts
    in the Bible, 21, 33
    nutritional value of, 20
    St. John's Bread, 38–39
    swarms of, 33–34

M
Marshmallows
    Termite Treats, 53
Martin, Daniella, 10, 83
Mealworms
    buying, 75–76
    cooking tips for, 77
    giant, 77
    Larval Latkes (a.k.a.
        Grubsteaks), 80
    measuring, 13, 77
    nutritional value of, 76
    raising, 15
    seasonal availability of, 12
    storing, 76
Mopane worms, 73–74
Mouffet, Thomas, 108
Mushrooms
    Cockroach à la King, 78–79
    Odonate Hors d'Oeuvres, 112

N
Nabhan, Gary, 12
Neuroptera. See Termites
Niblets and Cricklets, 25

O

Oaxacan Whoppers, 36
O'Brien, Conan, 22
Odonate Hors d'Oeuvres, 112
Orthoptera, 20–22. *See also* Crickets; Grasshoppers; Katydids
Orthopteran Orzo, 27

P

Pancakes
    Ant Jemima's Buckwheat-Bug Griddlecakes, 63
    Larval Latkes (a.k.a. Grubsteaks), 80
Party Pupae, 116
Pasta
    Orthopteran Orzo, 27
Pear Salad with Chiangbai Ants, 69
Pemberton, Robert W., 110
Pest-o, 90
Pineapple
    Bugs in a Rug, 31
    Sweet and Sour Silkworm, 105
Piz-zz-zz-za, 88–89

R

Really Hoppin' John, 43
Rennie, John, 32
Rice
    Really Hoppin' John, 43

S

St. John's Bread, 38–39
Salads
    Pear Salad with Chiangbai Ants, 69
    Three Bee Salad, 59
Saturniid moth pupae
    buying, 117
    cocoons of, 116
    Party Pupae, 116
    seasonal availability of, 12
Scorpions
    buying, 113
    harvesting, 113
    Scorpion Scaloppine, 113–15
    seasonal availability of, 12
    species of, 113
    stings from, 16, 115
    traveling with, 111

Sheeshi Kabobs, 41–42
Silkworm pupae
    life cycle of, 105
    nutritional value of, 4
    raising, 105
    Sweet and Sour Silkworm, 105
Sky Prawn, 110–11
Soups
    Alpha-Bait Soup, 91
    Cream of Katydid Soup, 35
Sow bugs, 12
Sphinx moth caterpillars, 116, 117
Spiders
    Deep-Fried Tarantula Spider, 119
    nutritional value of, 108
    as pets, 8
    species of, 108–9, 119
    Spin-akopita, 108–9
    stings from, 16
Spinach
    Pear Salad with Chiangbai Ants, 69
    Spin-akopita, 108–9
Stevens, Jane, 115
Superworms
    anatomy of, 84
    buying, 76
    measuring, 13, 77
    storing, 76–77
    Superworm Tempura with Plum Dipping Sauce, 84–85
Sweet and Sour Silkworm, 105
Sweet potatoes
    Larval Latkes (a.k.a. Grubsteaks), 80

T

Tavenner, Les, 56
Taylor, Ronald L., 8, 31, 60, 91, 93, 96, 113
Termites
    Curried Termite Stew, 52
    harvesting, 50, 51, 52
    nests of, 49–50, 51
    nutritional value of, 4, 51
    seasonal availability of, 12
    Termite Treats, 53
Three Bee Salad, 59
Tomatoes
    Fried Green Tomato Hornworms, 87
    Oaxacan Whoppers, 36

Piz-zz-zz-za, 88–89
    Sweet and Sour Silkworm, 105
Tomato hornworms
    Fried Green Tomato Hornworms, 87
    harvesting, 87
    life cycle of, 81–82
    seasonal availability of, 12
Tomberlin, Barney, 113
Torte, Chocolate Cricket, 32

V

Vidor, Brian, 21
Vij, Vikram, 30

W

Walnuts
    Bee's Knees, 60
    Chocolate Cricket Torte, 32
    Pest-o, 90
Wasabi Wax Worms, 83
Wasps, 16, 55, 56
Water bugs. *See* Giant water bugs
Watermelon and Water Bug Surprise, 103–4
Wax worms
    Alpha-Bait Soup, 91
    buying, 91
    cooking tips for, 83
    measuring, 13
    raising, 15
    seasonal availability of, 12
    Wasabi Wax Worms, 83
    White Chocolate and Wax Worm Cookies, 93
Weevils
    harvesting, 90
    nutritional value of, 4
    Pest-o, 90
Weissmann, Michael, 65
White Chocolate and Wax Worm Cookies, 93
Wines, 17
Wood, J. G., 20, 34, 49, 50, 77
Wu kung, 99

Z

Zucchini
    Oaxacan Whoppers, 36